THE SAGA SISTERS

Peter
best wishes & many thanks
Roy McCulla
Jan 2006

THE SAGA SISTERS

Clive Harvey & Roger Cartwright

TEMPUS

First published 2005

Tempus Publishing Ltd
The Mill, Brimscombe Port
Stroud, Gloucestershire GL5 2QG
www.tempus-publishing.com

British Library Cataloguing in Publication Data.
A catalogue record for this book is available from the British Library.

ISBN 0 7524 3418 7

Typesetting, design and origination by Tempus Publishing.
Printed in Great Britain

Contents

Norwegian America Line was the owner and operator of just eight liners during their seventy-six-year history. All of these ships acquired enviable reputations for service and style: whilst one was to become mostly renowned for her transatlantic voyages, the four post-war liners made their mark more as deluxe cruise ships; thereby ensuring Norwegian America Line recognition as one of the true elite cruise ship operators. Of this quartet *Sagafjord* and *Vistafjord*, the last two ships built for the Line, acquired legendary status. Their aura of glamour and grand luxe continued during their years with Cunard Line. Now these legendary sisters are again united under the ownership of Saga Cruises, as *Saga Rose* and *Saga Ruby*: the legend continues and this is their story.

Kristianafjord: Norwegian America Line's first liner, on her trials voyage off Gourock.

CHAPTER ONE

In the beginning

For the early emigrants, regardless of their country of origin, their journey to America was a hazardous one, in cramped conditions aboard a sailing vessel: the voyage taking several weeks. For many people in central European countries their journey began by rail, crossing several countries before reaching a port. Then, they may have been trans-shipped by some smaller vessel to another port before embarking upon a larger vessel to complete the voyage. By the mid-late 1800s transportation was by steamer, and even for those travelling from a country like Norway, with its strong maritime heritage, they were still reliant upon the major shipping lines of Britain and Germany to provide them with transoceanic transportation. The Norwegians would first cross the North Sea in a small steamer, to Newcastle or Hull, from where they would be taken to either Liverpool or Southampton to board either a Cunard or White Star liner for the voyage to New York. Alternatively, they would voyage down to Bremerhaven before boarding a Nord Deutscher Lloyd steamer to take them across the Atlantic.

There were those, however, who were anxious that Norway should establish a transatlantic steamship company of its own. In 1871 Peter Jebsen, a businessman, prominent in Bergen, established Det Norske-Amerikanske Dampskibsselskab (The Norwegian-American Steamship Company), and offered direct regular sailings from Bergen to New York, with modern purpose-built emigrant steamers. Sadly, unsatisfactory trading results meant that it turned out to be a short-lived venture. The service being abandoned in 1876, and the ships were employed in other trades. The Danish company, Thingvalla Line was initially rather more successful, probably because it also included calls in Sweden and Norway as well as Denmark. However, this company also got into financial difficulties and were eventually taken over in 1898 by the Danish United Steamship Company. Despite Peter Jebsen's failure the pressure still remained for there to be a Norwegian company operating an Atlantic service, and likewise, this was countered by the argument that the country was too small and too poor to make such a dream into a workable reality.

Even with the intense patriotic fervour that followed the dissolution of the unpopular union between Sweden and Norway in 1905, the idea of a national shipping line met with considerable resistance. At the time 800,000 Norwegians had already left for America, a figure that implied a national shipping line was needed, yet several well-known ship owners spoke out strongly against the idea: stating it to be an expensive and fool-hardy project. There was talk of a joint venture between the Scandinavian countries, but no agreement was ever reached between the companies involved, and the project quietly faded. However, in May 1910, plans for Norwegian America Line were presented to the public, with an invitation to subscribe to a share capital of 10 million Norwegian Kronor. The following February the first Board of Directors was elected, and Gustav Henriksen was appointed as the first managing director. Later that same year the contracts for two passenger liners were placed with the British yard, Cammell-Laird, Birkenhead. The vessels were scheduled to be delivered in 1913.

The new ships, both of 11,000gt, were given the names *Kristianafjord* and *Bergensfjord*, thus beginning a style of naming that continued until 1973 with the introduction of the company's final passenger liner, *Vistafjord*. *Kristianafjord* entered service in the spring, and was followed by her sister, several months later, in the autumn. Despite the view expressed by some, that the idea of a national shipping line was foolhardy, the success of the two ships passed all expectations, even those of their owners. Passengers that might have otherwise sailed with the DFDS-owned Scandinavian American Line chose to sail on the new Norwegian America Line ships instead, to such an extent that travellers aboard Scandinavian American were reduced to a minimum. It was clear to the Norwegian America management that a third ship was required. Again they turned to Cammell-Laird, and a contract was placed for a new 13,000 gt liner, to be completed in 1917.

Unfortunately, the turmoil of the First World War disrupted this plan, even though Norway remained neutral during the conflict. Also, despite their neutral stance it was inevitable that the country's ships would suffer as a result of mines, u-boat attacks and blocked trade routes. Luckily, however, only one of the companies' vessels was actually lost by direct war action (by this time they were also operators of a fleet of cargo vessels). To add to the problems generated by the war,

Crowds gather as *Stavangerfjord* prepares to sail from Oslo. The photograph was taken
in the late 1920s or early 1930s.

Kristianafjord was lost when she ran aground off Cape Race, in 1917. Once the war ended, the directors of NAL implemented a programme of considerable expansion. Orders were placed with both British and Canadian shipyards, for a total of six cargo liners, and by 1920 the line had a fleet of twelve vessels.

Stavangerfjord, the liner that had been originally scheduled to enter the company's service in 1917, was completed in April 1918 but moved from Birkenhead to New York, where she was laid-up. Once the war was over she made her first transatlantic voyage for the line in September, from New York to Oslo. Unfortunately, the restrictive immigration laws that the United States introduced in the early 1920s forced Norwegian America Line, along with all the other companies offering Atlantic services, to consider alternative employment for their ships. At the time it was seen as quite a problem, as the very reason that Norwegian America Line had been established in the first place was to essentially provide transportation for emigrants leaving the hardships of Norway to seek new lives in America. Nevertheless, the quota restrictions placed on emigrants entering the United States would prove to be a blessing in disguise for the still relatively fledgling company. It had been decided that both their two liners, *Bergensfjord* and *Stavangerfjord* would be sent on a series of cruises, and in 1925 the ships sailed on the first of these; to the North Cape, the fjords, Scotland, Iceland and to the Baltic Capitals. Whilst this was seen as a mod-est beginning it would ultimately become the activity for which Norwegian America Line would become most well known, and would acquire an enviable reputation for.

In 1935, the company marked the twenty-fifth anniversary of their founding by announcing that they were in the position to order a new passenger liner. In November of that year, when the plans and specifications had been drawn up, tenders were invited. Some of the major shipbuilders of the day came up with designs that met the company's specifications. Wilton-Fijenoord of Rotterdam, Adriatico at Monfalcone, Cammell Laird at Birkenhead, Swan Hunter at Newcastle and Fairfield of Glasgow: each of the yards producing designs for very similar looking liners of very restrained yet elegant lines. The design submitted by Adriatico being particularly favoured by the Norwegian America Line directors. However, given Italy's recent invasion of Ethiopia and the resulting League of Nations sanctions, placing the order with them was deemed inadvisable. The NAL directors reconsidered their options: both *Stavangerfjord* and *Bergensfjord* had received successful refitting work in Germany, and given the attractive financing, it was decided that the contract to build the new flagship would be awarded to Deschimag AG Weser of Bremen. The actual signing of the contract took place on 15 May 1936. Looking back, it is a curious irony that the Norwegian America Line directors were wary of placing the order with Fascist Italy but ended up placing it with Nazi Germany.

Reflections of the graceful and yacht-like *Bergensfjord*.

Even Third Class aboard *Bergensfjord* had a degree of elegance: the Third Class Lounge.

sailed from Oslo for the final time for New York. She then began her second programme of cruises down to the untroubled waters of the Caribbean. Meanwhile, her fleet mates continued the risky business of transatlantic sailings. In December 1939 *Stavangerfjord* was laid up in Oslo, leaving the oldest ship of the fleet, *Bergensfjord*, in Atlantic service. On 9 April 1940, when Germany invaded Norway, *Bergensfjord* was luckily at sea, on her way to New York. By this time, her series of Caribbean cruises at and end the new *Oslofjord* was laid-up in New York. It was the fate of *Stavangerfjord* to fall into the hands of the invading German troops.

After several months of inactivity *Oslofjord* left New York, on 26 October 1940, for Halifax, Nova Scotia. Then, having been repainted in shades of grey, at the end of November she sailed for England where she was to be converted into a troop transport. On 1 December, when she was off the river Tyne, approaching Newcastle, she struck a mine. It was the end of the virtually new liner, for although her crew managed to beach her off South Shields: she broke her back during subsequent bad weather. Her end being all the more tragic, as she had not even been able to contribute to the war effort. In November 1941 *Bergensfjord* was converted into a troopship at Halifax, NS, and sailed extensively in this role throughout the war. *Stavangerfjord* had been moved by the German forces from Oslo to the Trondheimfjord where

On 29 December 1937 the new ship was launched and was named *Oslofjord*. Six months later, on 4 June 1938, she made her maiden voyage, from Oslo and Bergen to New York. At 18,673 gross tons she was not a large ship, she was however, very handsome being beautifully proportioned with very simple and very modern lines. Curiously, despite her modernity, she had been fitted with the old-style quadrant davits. She was NAL's first motor liner and was at the time the largest geared, diesel-powered ship on the Atlantic. *Oslofjord* was very much a ship of the future: while her passengers were accommodated in three classes; 152 in Cabin, 307 in Tourist and 401in Third Class, she was designed with cruising very much in mind. The main Cabin and Tourist Class public rooms were on Promenade Deck and were so designed to be opened up to one class cruising, and the light and airy décor enhanced this. During the winter of 1938-1939 the ship operated a series of Caribbean and South America cruises from New York. These were a great success and a further similar programme was planned for the following winter. World events, however, ensured that this was not to be.

In September 1939 Europe, and then much of the rest of the World was plunged into the turmoil of another war. Norway once again remained neutral and for a while *Oslofjord*, *Stavangerfjord* and *Bergensfjord* continued with their regular North Atlantic service, each liner boldly painted with neutrality markings on their hulls. The ships were kept busy on the westward run, full of passengers fleeing to the safety of America. Neutrality markings were, however, no sure guarantee of safety with the unrestricted activity of the submarines in the Atlantic. On 4 October 1939 *Oslofjord*

The romantic image of the transatlantic voyage. The parasol would have been an unlikely accessory on this, the Third Class Promenade, forward aboard *Stavangerfjord*.

The Second Class Smoke Room aboard *Stavangerfjord* also doubled as a Ballroom.

Norwegian America Line evokes Norway's maritime heritage in its promotion of its magnificent new liner, *Stavangerfjord*.

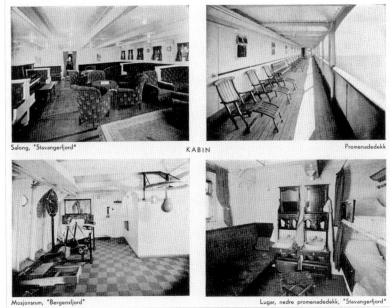

Stavangerfjord: First Class Lounge; Promenade Deck; Gymnasium; Cabin.

The simple modern appearance of the 1938 *Oslofjord* initiated a style that would become a Norwegian America Line trademark.

she served as an accommodation ship for the German Navy. With the retreat of the German forces from Norway, *Stavangerfjord* was recovered in May 1945 and was found to be in an appallingly neglected state. Nevertheless, useful passenger ships were at a premium at this desperate time: displaced persons, war brides and immigrants all anxiously seeking to leave war-torn Europe; thus *Stavangerfjord* was hastily refitted to be able to operate an austerity service. She departed on the first of these repatriation voyages in September 1945, sailing from Oslo for New York.

The loss of the *Oslofjord* had been a severe blow to Norwegian America, as it left them, twenty-seven years after the end of the First World War, in exactly the same position they had been in back in 1918, with the same two liners. *Bergensfjord* was by this time thirty-two-years old and the company decided that her age combined with her hard use during the years of war made her no longer suitable for further NAL service. She was placed in lay-up in June 1945, after having been visited by His Majesty King Haakon VII. Whilst deemed unsuitable for NAL service, her career was far from over. The *Bergensfjord* was sold the following February to the fledgling Home Lines and sailed for them as the *Argentina*. Later she would see service as the *Jerusalem* for another new company, the Zim Israel Line, remaining in service until 1959.

Norwegian America Line was reduced to just the one liner, *Stavangerfjord*, and after her brief re-entry into service as an austerity liner she was sent in early 1946 to a Swedish shipyard to be fully refitted: the work taking until May to be completed. She resumed transatlantic service on the last day of that month.

Bergensfjord on the Clyde on 4 May 1946, shortly before she sailed from Bergen to become Home Lines' *Argentina*.

Oslofjord and Bergensfjord

May 1946 was a significant month for Norwegian America Line. The refurbishment and modernisation of *Stavangerfjord* completed, the liner sailed on 31 May for New York. However, on 1 May the company had signed a contract with N.V. Nederlandsche Dok en Sheepbouw Maatschappij of Amsterdam (otherwise known as the Netherlands Dock & Shipbuilding Co.) for the construction of a new twin-screw motor-ship.

In fact, despite the pressures of war, Norwegian America Line had commenced working out plans for a new liner in the autumn of 1942, confident in their determination that once those dark days of war were over they would be able to continue their transatlantic traffic. The plans contemplated a vessel of 16,000 tons displacement and with accommodation for 550 passengers in two classes. The service speed was stipulated to be 19 knots. These plans were discussed at some length and some alterations were made, and following the German surrender a preliminary specification with plans was sent to some of the leading shipbuilding yards in Europe to get some indication of price levels and the time of delivery. By the end of 1945 a complete specification, final plans and a profile of the liner were worked out by Norwegian America and negotiations began with some of the shipyards offering the most favourable terms: the contract ultimately being awarded to the Netherlands Dock & Shipbuilding Co.

In a report made at the time the order was placed, it was stated that 'The vessel will have very fine lines with a well-raked stem in order to obtain a constant angle of approach. She will have a cruiser stern with a large overhang so as to provide a good length on the water line. The bottom will be strengthened in excess of requirements, bearing in mind the hard service on the North Atlantic and a good flare will be give to the fore body.'

The yard of the Netherlands Dock & Shipbuilding Co. was almost completely destroyed during the war; even the berths had been damaged, so it was virtually necessary to build a new shipyard. The reconstruction of the yard was hastened by the fact that many men, skilled shipbuilders and engineers, helped in this work and as a result the shipyard was able to function much sooner than had been expected.

However, it was not until March 1948 that the keel of what would become the second *Oslofjord* was laid, late delivery of material having further handicapped the builders.

Electric arc welding was extensively used in the construction of the ship and her shell plating was partly welded and partly riveted. The wheel house, bridge front and the funnel of the new ship were constructed of aluminium alloy. The initial plan for her to accommodate 200 passengers in Cabin Class and 370 in Tourist was revised before the ship was completed to 266 in what was renamed First Class, and 359 in Tourist. Considerable effort was made to make the ship as soundproof and fire-proof as possible, with much use made of asbestos plates for the bulkheads dividing the cabins. The ship was designed not only to carry passengers but also with the facility to transport cargo. She had five holds, three forward and two aft, with a capacity of about 230,000 cubic ft. This was used for the transportation of frozen fish to the United States. Like her predecessor, she was a motor ship, powered by Stork diesels, which would give her a service speed of 20 knots, although on trials she would achieve a maximum in excess of 21 knots.

2 April 1949 was a gala day in Amsterdam, a day charged with excitement and international goodwill. The pearl grey hull of the *Oslofjord* appeared to dominate the flat Dutch countryside for miles around. She was, at that time, the largest liner to be built in Holland for a foreign owner. Shortly after noon several thousand spectators had gathered to watch the partially completed liner take to the water for the first time. Crown Prince Olav and his wife Crown Princess Martha had arrived from Oslo, and it was the Crown Princess who would perform the naming ceremony. They had been welcomed by Queen Juliana and Prince Bernhard, and later met Pieter Goedkoop, the managing director of the shipbuilding company. Flags of both Norway and Holland decorated the canopied stand from which the Crown Princess would perform the naming ceremony. As the Royal party gathered at the flag-deck stand they were joined by city officials and members of the diplomatic corps, directors of the shipyard and from Norwegian America Line: amongst them

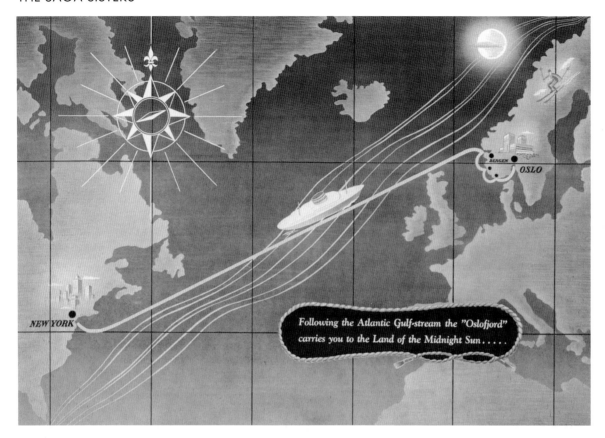

Following the Atlantic Gulf-stream the "Oslofjord" carries you to the Land of the Midnight Sun.....

Norwegian America Line implies a warm and calm crossing for the 1949 *Oslofjord* by invoking the Gulf Stream.

was Kaare Haug who had been responsible for the design of the ship. The harbour was alive with sightseeing craft. At 3 p.m. Crown Princess Martha stepped forward and said "Thy name shall be *Oslofjord*, may good luck and prosperity follow thee upon the high seas." The words spoken, a bottle of champagne was released and smashed against the pristine hull and below the chain of events set to release the ship fell into place. The crowds roared as gradually the flag-decked hull began to move and within just forty-three seconds Norwegian America Line's new flagship was afloat. With *Oslofjord* safely launched tugs slipped alongside and nudged her slowly and carefully into a nearby berth, where months of outfitting would prepare her for entry into luxury transatlantic and cruise service.

Work on the fitting out of the *Oslofjord* proceeded rapidly and she was ready to run her technical trials voyage in October, just six months after her launching. During these trials some fairly rough weather was encountered and her designers and builders were well satisfied with her sea-keeping qualities. On 11 November she left Amsterdam for her homeport of Oslo, with 250 guests aboard. On her

arrival the whole city seemed to have turned out to give a fitting welcome to what was Norway's new national flagship.

While the public rooms and other accommodations of *Oslofjord* possessed that degree of luxury that was expected of a transatlantic liner of that time, the decorative scheme was exceptionally pleasing throughout and a distinct Norwegian atmosphere had been created. Norwegian America had given the responsibility for the interior design to a Dutch architect and the architect of Oslo City Hall (a building that was then nearing completion). They also commissioned some of Norway's leading artists to provide paintings, ceramic mosaics and tapestries for the lounges and dining rooms. As with the previous *Oslofjord*, the whole of the promenade deck had been allocated to the chief public rooms, with Tourist Class being served equally as well as First Class.

On 26 November 1949 *Oslofjord* sailed for New York on her 'official' maiden voyage. Her transatlantic service included calls at Copenhagen, Kristiansand, Stavanger, and Bergen. In the winter of 1951 she re-introduced Norwegian

A simple but evocative advertisement for Norwegian America Line from an early 1950s issue of the *National Geographic* magazine.

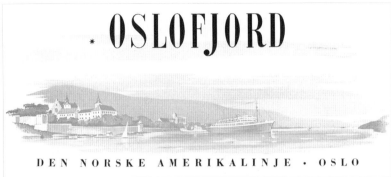

Norwegian America Line introduces the new *Oslofjord*.

Even while under construction *Oslofjord* appeared strikingly modern.

America's cruises from New York to the Caribbean. The following year, on 9 February 1952, she sailed from New York on a long cruise to the Mediterranean, and this was to become a regular feature of her cruise schedule. To make her more attractive as a cruise ship a portable swimming pool would be fitted into one of the hatches leading down to an aft cargo hold (she also had a permanent indoor pool down on E Deck). During a refit in 1953, in order to make her even more suited to tropical cruising, her partial air-conditioning was extended throughout the ship. For the next several years her pattern of service would be that she would spend about nine months on the North Atlantic route, in tandem with the now ageing but still highly popular, *Stavangerfjord*, then in the winter months with her passenger capacity reduced to a mere 390, she would undertake a series of cruises. These cruises were sometimes lengthy and exotic, including calls in Africa or South America as well as the long Mediterranean cruise. In June 1956 *Oslofjord* diverted from her regular Atlantic service and instead made a 40-day cruise out of New York to the North Cape and the Norwegian fjords. The popularity of the cruise was such that she repeated it for several years and thus the dye was cast for the future operation of the ships of the Norwegian America Line.

Even before *Oslofjord* had sailed on this 40-day odyssey she had met with considerable success in both her North Atlantic service as well as a cruise ship, and spurred on by this success Norwegian America put in hand plans for another liner: similar but larger. Once again the task of designing this new ship was entrusted to Kaare Haug. His design of the new ship followed closely that of the *Oslofjord*, with similar curving superstructure and a graceful hull form. The contract to build the ship was awarded to Swan, Hunter & Wigham Richardson, Ltd, of Wallsend. The fact that they had won this prestigious contract was a cause for considerable congratulation as there had been keen competition from other European shipbuilders. The new flagship was to revive the name *Bergensfjord*, and she was

The crowds roared as the flag-decked hull slid down the launch way.

Crown Princess Martha and the official party watch anxiously.

launched on 18 July 1955, the naming ceremony being performed by her Royal Highness Princess Astrid.

Bergensfjord was the largest ship to have been completed by the Swan, Hunter shipyard since the war. She was a ship of many outstanding features but perhaps the most important was the extensive aluminium-alloy superstructure, which was principally of welded fabricated construction. The connection of this aluminium structure to the steel hull of the ship was by means of galvanised bolts and Neoprene packing, which was used to minimise any corrosion. This was at the time the largest aluminium superstructure created for a European-built passenger liner. Although *Bergensfjord* bore a strong resemblance to the *Oslofjord*, her superstructure was longer in order to give her a greater array of passenger facilities, and her graceful lines and streamlined superstructure met with considerable approval by the shipping industry press and the travelling public alike. She had eight decks: Sports, Upper, Sun, Promenade, A, B, C and D and copying the prevailing mood of the times, there was accommodation for just 100 passengers in First Class and 775 in Tourist Class. Her crew numbered 335, giving her a total compliment of 1,210. Her Tourist Class cabins were the equivalent of First Class on many of the ships then employed on the Atlantic, all of them being fitted with private toilets and all but a small proportion of them had either a bath or shower as well. The ship also had the facility to carry cargo, 100,000 cubic ft of it and this was contained in the holds, two forward and one aft, together with their associated 'tween deck spaces.

Whilst *Oslofjord* had proved to be a very popular and successful cruise ship during the winter months, *Bergensfjord* was designed and built to be principally employed on the Scandinavia to New York route. This was the period when the 'Atlantic ferry' was in its most successful period of all time, and the transatlantic liners were filled on almost every voyage. With the entry of *Bergensfjord* into service Norwegian America Line would have three liners on the Oslo, Copenhagen New York run. However, Norwegian America were forward thinking in the design of their new liner in that the *Oslofjord* had indicated for them the potential growth of the cruise market. So, unlike many other companies at that time, they had her

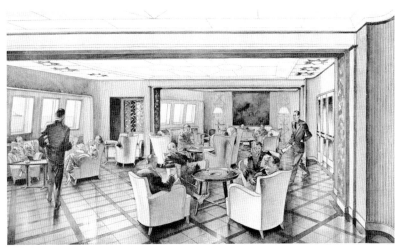

The forward-facing First Class Smoking Room: described in publicity material of the time as 'having its own gay cocktail bar'.

The Tourist Class Dining Room: Tourist Class aboard *Oslofjord* was as well appointed as First Class on many other companies.

THE GARDEN LOUNGE — One of the most delightful spots on the *Oslofjord* is this glass enclosed room which encompasses the entire forward end of the *Promenade Deck*. Here, on every side, you enjoy an unobstructed view of the open sea. There are fresh flowers in the vases, and green plants growing, and cheerfulness in the air. Try it and see for yourself.

Above: A First Class Suite, elegant and stylish: *Oslofjord* set the trend that other Norwegian America Liners would follow.

Left: The Garden Lounge – a feature that would appear in each subsequent Norwegian America liner.

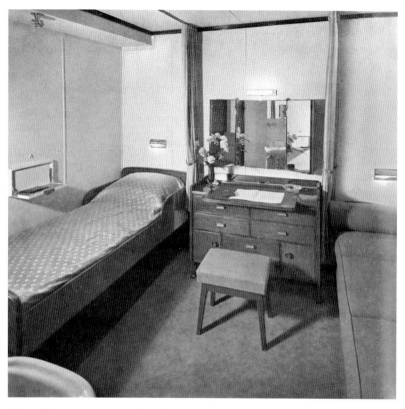

A First Class stateroom: simple and modern yet very attractive.

was just aft of the forward-facing lounge. There was, however, a further lounge known as the 'Club Bergen, located forward on Sun Deck. With its large windows giving a view out over the bows this was certainly the most attractive room on the ship. However, for sheer splendour one could not have failed to be impressed by the Tourist Class dining room. This room, the centre section of which was two decks high, would not have been out of place in First Class. The forward end of this magnificent room was dominated by a huge painting, which reached to the ceiling, entitled 'The Dream Voyage.'

Bergensfjord was powered by two Stork double-acting, two-stroke cycle, eight-cylinder diesel engines that had been manufactured in Holland. These gave her a service speed of 20 knots though a maximum of 22.1 knots had been achieved during her trials, which had been held on 9 April. Even though the building work on *Bergensfjord* had begun ten years after the end of the war there was still a shortage of steel and labour. Despite these difficulties Swan, Hunter managed to complete the ship a whole month ahead of schedule, on 14 May 1956. Her delivery from the river Tyne took her first to Bergen – her homeport – to Stavanger and Kristiansand before arriving in Oslo on Norway's Independence Day, 17 May. It was from Oslo that she sailed, on 30 May, on her maiden voyage to New York. On her arrival, on 9 June, she was met with considerable praise and was an immediate success. With

designed with the facility to be adaptable to 'off season' cruising. The consideration of her potential as a cruise ship was the reasoning behind the decision to fit out the passenger accommodation to a higher standard than was normally found on the Atlantic. Also a number of her public rooms had been designed for dual-purpose use. Another facility to make the ship fully suited to a cruising role was that she was fully air-conditioned.

Arnstein Arneberg, who at the time was one of the best-known Norwegian architects, was contracted to plan the interior of *Bergensfjord*, and the decoration of the public rooms was carried out by Hampton & Sons Ltd, and Maple & Co. Ltd. The decoration was in the Scandinavian style using Norwegian traditions as the decorative theme. While there was considerable use of handsome wood panelling the furnishings were generally light in colour and extensive use was made of tapestries, paintings and decorative glass panelling. Again, following the design layout of the *Oslofjord* and her predecessor, all the principal public rooms were on Promenade deck, including the relatively intimate First Class dining room, which

Despite her relatively modest tonnage *Oslofjord* gave her First Class passengers a dining room every bit as grand as those aboard the transatlantic giants.

Norwegian America Line now able to boast a fleet of three liners, albeit that one was the elderly but exceptionally popular *Stavangerfjord*, they were able to increase their cruise programme. When in her role as a cruise ship *Bergensfjord*'s passenger capacity was reduced to just 420 in one class. So few on a liner of just under 19,000 gross tons must have created a very special aura of exclusivity about her cruises. Her first cruises were scheduled to start just six months after her entry into service and took her to Bermuda, Nassau and the Caribbean.

With their fleet once again restored to three ships, two of which were very modern, Norwegian America temporarily withdrew the 38-year-old *Stavangerfjord* from service in order for her to be extensively upgraded. The contract for this work was also awarded to the Swan, Hunter yard, and surprisingly at this late stage in her career, stabilisers were fitted. The initial plan had been that upon *Bergensfjord*'s entry into service *Stavangerfjord* would be withdrawn altogether. However, with the Atlantic trade booming at that time she was given the life-extending refit instead. With the much up-graded *Stavangerfjord* maintaining the year-round Atlantic service Norwegian America were in the position of being able to offer an even more extensive cruise programme than before. What was entitled Norwegian America Line's 'Carefree Cruises' took *Bergensfjord* to South America, Africa and right around the world, and this firmly established the line in the luxury cruise market.

During November and December 1957 *Oslofjord* underwent extensive refitting work. Like her fleet mates, she was also fitted with stabilisers. Also, to bring her in line with her younger sister several of her cabins were upgraded by the inclusion of private bathrooms. With the two ships now offering comparable accommodation they were every bit as luxurious as their close rivals, the *Kungsholm* and *Gripsholm* of Swedish America Line that were also operating lengthy wintertime cruises from New York. The refreshing light modernity of the Scandinavian liners, coupled with a high standard of on board service even managed to lure passengers away from the likes of the well-established yet somewhat more grand, *Caronia* of Cunard Line. In 1958 the numbers of people crossing the Atlantic by ship reached a peak of 1,030,000. At this same time the first commercial jet aircraft was introduced between Europe and New York. While this did make an immediate effect on the numbers travelling by sea the numbers steadied and for a year or two remained at around 800,000. Luckily both *Oslofjord* and *Bergensfjord* were well able to cope being ideally suited to a cruising role. Now their transatlantic sailings were more and more interspersed with summertime cruises, and their lovely profiles were to be seen gracing the ports of the Mediterranean, the Baltic and their home waters of the Norwegian fjords.

By 1960 Norwegian America were beginning to consider plans for another new liner: indeed, in order that they retain their position at the luxury end of the cruise market a new ship was essential. After all, by this time *Oslofjord* was over ten years old and the venerable *Stavangerfjord*, though still a much loved ship, at over

40-years old, was the oldest liner on the North Atlantic. She was retained in the fleet until 1963. She made her final departure from New York on 3 December, with fire boats sending up plumes of water in salute and crowds on onlookers as she headed down the Hudson for the last time. Whilst there had been some moves to preserve the liner she was in fact sold to the Shun Fung Iron Works at Hong Kong, to be broken up; and she arrived there on 4 February 1964. The withdrawal of the *Stavangerfjord* in effect ended Norwegian America Line's regular Atlantic service, for both *Oslofjord* and *Bergensfjord* were by this time only operating a summer Atlantic service and even that was occasionally broken by one of the ships diverting to a mid-summer cruise.

By this time in fact, Norwegian America had begun to give some thought to the future of the *Oslofjord*. For although she had been designed with, to some extent, a

Bergensfjord: perfection afloat.

cruising role in mind, she was, compared to *Bergensfjord* and the soon to be delivered new flagship, rather more of a transatlantic liner. She was in effect, outclassed by her fleet mates, and this was all the more apparent once the new ship was delivered. In 1966 there were rumours that *Oslofjord* was for sale and it was said that Finnlines wanted her for their planned entry into the cruise trade. Nothing came of this however. To ensure her continued operation out of the United States under the new 1966 Fire Safety Regulations, and probably to enhance her potential sale value, Norwegian America sent her back to her builders in November 1966 for a three-month refit. This would update her safety equipment, provide additional cabin facilities and extend her Promenade deck aft in order to provide a new, and permanent, pool and enhanced lido facilities. *Oslofjord* returned to service with

revised accommodation for 179 First Class and 469 Tourist class passengers. These figures were revised to just 450 when she was cruising, and the intention was that as a result of this refit she would now spend most of her time doing just that.

On 20 October 1967 *Oslofjord* left New York on her last Atlantic crossing to Oslo, a charter to Greek Line, for a series of cruises out of Southampton had been announced thereby cancelling all her 1968 Norwegian America line scheduled sailings. Her first cruise as part of this charter was a Christmas cruise to the Canary Islands. Although under charter to Greek Line the cruises were made under the Norwegian America Line name and with the ship in NAL colours. The cruises were a great success. However, the charter was only for one year and in October 1968 she was laid up in Oslo. Norwegian America was anxious to find

MAIN LOUNGE - TOURIST CLASS   DINING ROOM - FIRST CLASS

Bergensfjord followed the new trend in being a mainly Tourist Class liner, her grandly proportioned two-deck-high Tourist Class Dining Room was a reflection of this.

Bergensfjord's expansive deck areas meant that she was well suited for both Atlantic service and cruising: First Class Sports Deck.

STATEROOM - FIRST CLASS   SUITE

Above: The new *Bergensfjord* was decorated in an understated but very modern way: Tourist Class Main Lounge: First Class Dining Room.

Left: First Class Stateroom and First Class Suite.

Below right: Enclosed Promenade Deck.

Oslofjord at Oslo.

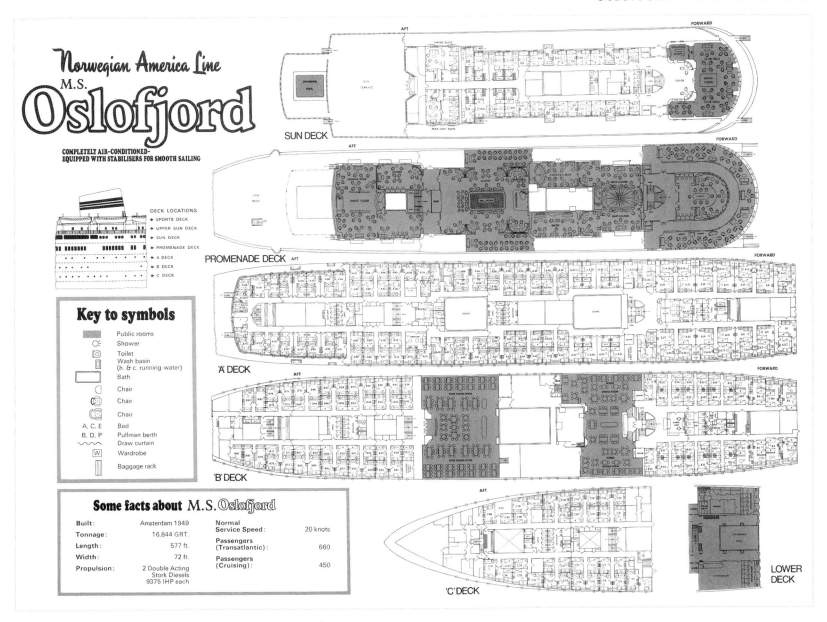

Norwegian America Line
M.S. Oslofjord

COMPLETELY AIR-CONDITIONED-
EQUIPPED WITH STABILISERS FOR SMOOTH SAILING

DECK LOCATIONS
- SPORTS DECK
- UPPER SUN DECK
- SUN DECK
- PROMENADE DECK
- A DECK
- B DECK
- C DECK

SUN DECK

PROMENADE DECK

'A' DECK

'B' DECK

'C' DECK

LOWER DECK

Key to symbols

	Public rooms
	Shower
	Toilet
	Wash basin (h. & c. running water)
	Bath
	Chair
	Chair
	Chair
A, C, E	Bed
B, D, P	Pullman berth
	Draw curtain
W	Wardrobe
	Baggage rack

Some facts about M.S. Oslofjord

Built :	Amsterdam 1949	Normal Service Speed :	20 knots
Tonnage :	16,844 GRT.	Passengers (Transatlantic) :	660
Length :	577 ft.	Passengers (Cruising) :	450
Width :	72 ft.		
Propulsion :	2 Double Acting Stork Diesels 9375 IHP each		

A Deck Plan of *Oslofjord* showing her arrangement after the 1966 refit.

Promoting *Oslofjord*'s cruises from Southampton.

Her sweeping lines gave *Oslofjord* a yacht-like appearance.

Although with longer superstructure, *Bergensfjord* was very similar to *Oslofjord*.

either a long-term charter or a buyer for the ship. As the year came to an end it seemed that she might be chartered to a British company, Ensco Shipping, for the Liverpool-Montreal service, but nothing ever came of this idea. Then, in May 1969, a three-year charter from Italy's Costa line was secured, and it seemed that at the end of the charter they had every intention of buying the ship.

Though still under Norwegian registry and with Norwegian officers, *Oslofjord* adopted the more Italian-sounding name *Fulvia*. Her hull was painted white with a blue line and her funnel a deep yellow with the large "C" logo of Costa Line, in dark blue. She sailed that December from Oslo for the Caribbean. In San Juan she joined her new fleetmates, *Flavia* and *Federico C*, making weekly circuits to St Thomas, Martinique, Trinidad, La Guaira and Curacao. *Fulvia* returned to Europe in June 1970 to begin a series of ten cruises that would include Mediterranean ports as well as the Atlantic Islands. She sailed from Genoa on 14 July on what should have been another routine cruise out to the Canary Islands. Sadly, she would never complete this cruise.

Promoted as the ultimate in luxury afloat: the First Class Lounge aboard *Oslofjord*.

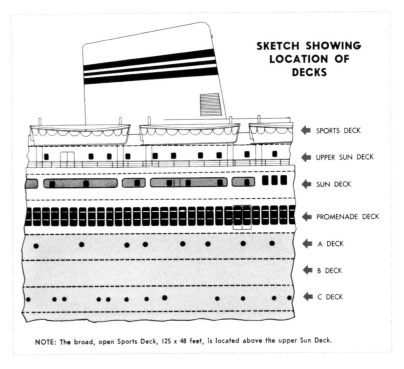

SKETCH SHOWING LOCATION OF DECKS

◄ SPORTS DECK

◄ UPPER SUN DECK

◄ SUN DECK

◄ PROMENADE DECK

◄ A DECK

◄ B DECK

◄ C DECK

NOTE: The broad, open Sports Deck, 125 x 48 feet, is located above the upper Sun Deck.

Oslofjord in Southampton.

Some of *Bergensfjord*'s stewards and stewardesses posed on her aft deck.

In the early hours of 19 July, when she was sailing between Funchal and Tenerife, there was an explosion in her generator room. This started a fire that very quickly spread from the engine room and threatened to engulf the whole ship. Her 445 passengers were given the order to abandon ship at 4.30 a.m. and *Fulvia*'s SOS message was picked up by the French liner *Ancerville*. Two hours later the lifeboats, with all the passengers and crew aboard, left the blazing liner and were taken aboard the French ship. *Fulvia* developed a list to port and a Spanish tug tried to take her in tow while fire-fighting vessels sprayed her with water. It was a pointless task. The former pride of the Norwegian merchant marine was dead. Reduced to a charred and twisted hulk, she sank in the early afternoon of 20 July 1970.

CHAPTER THREE

Sagafjord

Whilst Norwegian America Line's plans for a new liner had begun to take shape during the summer of 1960, during 1961 they gathered real momentum. It had been decided, at a very early stage, that because of the vagaries of the weather on the most northerly of the North Atlantic routes (which the Scandinavian Atlantic liners took when voyaging to and from New York) the new vessel would be primarily employed for cruising, based on New York. The plan being that for as much as 10 ½ months she would operate as a cruise ship with her Atlantic service being restricted to voyages to and from Norway for annual overhaul and refitting and major crew changes. The design of the ship was therefore basically as a one-class vessel with a layout that would easily permit a simple conversion into a two-class arrangement when working under the North Atlantic Conference rules. On 24 September 1962, the contract to build the ship was awarded to Societe des Forges et Chantiers de la Mediterranee, which was located at La Seyne Sur Mer, near Toulon. The contract was a fixed price, in the region of NK100 million (approximately £5 million). While Mr Leif Hoegh, the chairman of Norwegian America had a forty per cent interest in the ship the French Government subsidised the builders to the extent of seventeen per cent of the labour costs, which probably amounted to twenty-five per cent of the contract price. As it would turn out, of the total cost about twenty per cent was accounted for by machinery, split equally between propulsion engines and auxiliaries, the air conditioning two per cent, and the interior decorating thirteen per cent — almost double the budget figure!

The plans were drawn for the ship by Norwegian America's own marine architects and engineers — principally being the work of Mr Kaare Haug — and they designed a ship that, while very similar in general appearance to both her more recent fleet mates, was quite a radical departure in many ways from other ships being built at that time. On 19 June 1963 the first plates of the ship were laid down and for some while it was seriously speculated that she just might break with tradition and be named *Norway*. A workforce of over 1,300 were employed on constructing the ship: not just the French shipbuilders but the architects and engineers from Norwegian America's technical department, along with artisans from the Netherlands, Belgium, Italy, Sweden and Denmark. During the design stages efficiency and sea-keeping qualities of the hull form were tested at the Norwegian High School testing tank in Trondheim. The tests were undertaken with both a bulbous bow and with a more conventional bow. Bearing in mind the speed requirements, and with the full knowledge of the efficiency of the similarly shaped *Oslofjord* and *Bergensfjord*, it was decided that the bulbous bow offered no significant advantage.

The launching of the partially completed ship was set for 13 June 1964, and this was to be held without ceremony. Speculation that she might carry the name *Norway* was unfounded as the name *Sagafjord* was there on her hull.

At that time the use of aluminium was very popular in the construction of the upper works of passenger liners as it is much lighter in weight than steel; and 520 tons of the material, mined from near Les Baux where Bauxite, from which aluminium is derived, was first discovered, was used to construct the entire superstructure of *Sagafjord*, from weather deck to funnel. *Sagafjord* was powered by two Sulzer diesel engines, coupled direct to twin screws, which were designed to propel the liner at 20 knots while utilising only sixty-five per cent of her 24,000 total horsepower. On 7 May 1965 she was ready to run her first sea trials: fitting out of the liner continued during the following summer months. On 4 September she sailed on her final sea trials over the French Navy's measured mile, off Toulon. It was during these trials *Sagafjord* registered a speed of 21.7 knots utilising only eighty-two per cent of her power and she achieved a maximum of 22.5 knots, which was well in excess of her designed cruising speed. This splendid achievement was sadly rather overshadowed by the fact that *Sagafjord* had been completed six months behind schedule, thereby missing a very lucrative summer season of Atlantic crossings and cruises. The delay was also a devastating blow to the shipyard — as the ship had been constructed on a fixed-price contract.

Despite the delay nothing could detract from the fact that *Sagafjord* was a ship of considerable elegance and beauty: a flagship that Norwegian America Line

A striking view of *Sagafjord* as she is made ready for launching.

could be justly proud of. On 18 September the official naming ceremony of the *Sagafjord* was held, and Mrs Leif Hoegh, the wife of the Chairman of the Line was the sponsor.

At 24,002 gross tons, *Sagafjord* was Norwegian America's largest vessel; and she was both the largest passenger vessel, and the first North Atlantic vessel, to be constructed by her builders. Her overall length was 620ft and she was 82ft wide. On those rare occasions that she was to be employed on the North Atlantic run her passenger capacity would be 789 (seventy in First Class and 719 in Tourist Class). However, she would normally carry far fewer than that during her principal employment on lengthy cruises: just 450. A fact that really goes to emphasise that Norwegian America were very focussed on the luxury end of the cruise market (elsewhere these passenger capacity figures are quoted as being 817 when in transatlantic service and 462 while cruising). Kaare Haug had no belief in the unconventional just for the sake of it. *Sagafjord* was, in fact, a very conventional ship nevertheless in all her technical features every advantage was taken of the latest advances and practice. As with her exterior appearance, her internal décor was similarly restrained, bowing to neither extreme, yet providing both a modern and relaxing atmosphere. Ninety per cent of *Sagafjord's* cabins were outside; equally, ninety per cent were provided with full baths, the remainder having showers. There were four suites; the Fridtjof Nansen suite and Roald Amundsen suite, which were located on Sun Deck, and the Henrik Ibsen suite and Olav Trygvason suite on Upper Deck. There were a wide range of double and single cabin types, and many of them had interconnecting doors thereby allowing even further flexibility. The décor of the cabins and suites was very similar being a blend of warm wood veneer and cheerful pastel coloured walls, which were accented by colourful draperies.

Sagafjord had nine decks: Bridge, Sun, Veranda, Upper, Main, A, B, C and D Decks. Veranda Deck consisted entirely of public rooms, with the Garden Lounge being right forward. *Sagafjord* was a showcase of all that was the very best in Scandinavian interior design, and the Copenhagen-based architect Kay Korbing designed the Garden Lounge. He had already made his name designing very striking interiors of several DFDS vessels. The room was cleverly designed to have a circular appearance and had a sunken dance floor of white Italian marble. Gold anodised stanchions separated the central section of the room from the raised outer area, and this outer area was furnished with modern cane chairs. During the day the whole room was flooded with light from the broad sweep of windows. Aft of this room on the port side was the North Cape Bar whilst on the starboard side was the library and the writing room. The bar, which was panelled in palisander, was decorated in a similar style to the lounge and was enhanced by three large wood relief carvings. The library was circular and at the forward end of the writing room. When used as a two-class Atlantic liner these three spaces would be dedicated to First Class, being separated from the rest of the public rooms by a broad

Bottom: The old and the new. Cunard's *Caronia* meets *Sagafjord* in Hamburg, both ships on long cruises from New York to Northern Europe.

foyer across the width of the ship. In the space between the bar and the library/writing room was the 240-seat cinema, which had been designed by Gorges Peynet who had very recently designed the theatre aboard the liner *France*.

The 8,073sq. ft main lounge/ballroom was regarded as one of the most attractive rooms aboard the ship. Designed by Finn Nilsson, the room had a 14ft 6in centre section that extended the full length of the room and had only four pillars. A mural by Torstlin Riten was on the forward bulkhead and formed a back-drop to the stage and polished palisander dance floor. There was ample seating for all the passengers on dark blue-green upholstered settees and yellow cushioned pale grey steel chairs set on a rich two-tone red carpet: the full length curtains were yellow and gold. The glazed after end of the room looked on to the Verandah Café: also designed by Finn Nilsson. This in turn overlooked the outdoor swimming pool and lido deck through full height glass doors capable of being folded right back when the weather permitted.

On the Sun Deck, above the after end of the Main Lounge, was the dual-purpose Club Polaris, designed by Han van Tienhoven of Holland. Complete with its own galley, this room served as the First Class Dining Saloon when operating on the transatlantic service, or as a nightclub when the vessel was cruising. The club was isolated from the passenger cabins in order that night-time entertainments did not disturb anyone. The free standing charcoal grey bar was backed with a mirror-mounted varicoloured heavy glass mosaic by van der Broek, while the surface of the unusual dance floor was a chequerboard composed of copper and stainless steel squares each inset with a circle of the alternate metal. Directly over the dance floor were spotlights that were able to produce a variety of coloured effects. The walls of the room were panelled in alternating strips of silver and gold anodised aluminium. The windows were covered with hand-woven silk from Thailand that matched the red carpet. As with several of *Sagafjord*'s public rooms, the after bulkhead was completely glazed, and in this case overlooked the sports deck.

Sagafjord: the long-distance cruise ship, passing through the Panama Canal locks.

On the Main Deck was the magnificent Saga dining room; this followed the same structural pattern as the main lounge — single deck height to the sides of the room with a full-length two-deck high central section. The décor of the room was restrained and featured a red carpet, white walls, which on the sides and forward end were broken by niches housing designs of white concave and convex pyramid tiles that relied purely on light and shadow for their effect with wall lights to illuminate the designs in red or white to suit the hour and mood. The décor and furnishings of the room were by Fritjof S. Platou and Njaal Eide. The after two-deck high section was of plate glass and the grand staircase was viewed through this, as was the background decoration, by Carl B. Gunnarson, of gold finished forged iron, based on an old Norse stone carving, on a red mounting. Platou also designed the indoor swimming pool, on C Deck.

The works of many internationally known artists contributed greatly to *Sagafjord*'s interiors. Sigurd Winge executed the principal work of art aboard the ship: an abstract free-form design of vivid enamel hues on copper, entitled 'The Wind and the Signs.' It decorated as panel 25ft long and 6ft high located in the main foyer between the entrances to the cinema, on Veranda Deck. It is one of the three original pieces of artwork to remain aboard the ship. The other two are the heavy glass mosaic, by van den Broek, which lends a brilliant array of colour to the wall behind the indoor swimming pool and the Carl B. Gunnarson forged iron sculpture at the head of the staircase leading to the ding room (though this is now on a blue background).

Sagafjord's crew of 350 were provided with exceptionally good accommodation. All officers of the deck and engine departments were quartered on the Bridge Deck, in outside cabins and the officers' smoke room and mess was also situated on this deck. The rest of the crew were accommodated forward in the ship and along the entire B Deck, mostly in single and two-berth cabins.

In an interview Kaare Haug described *Sagafjord* as a 'rationalised ship'. He explained that rationalisation meant that the emphasis in the ship's design was on the convenient and orderly placement of various functions so as to eliminate waste. By this emphasis he was able to reduce the number of crew by 70 – to 350 – from what a ship of her size would ordinarily require. For example, the ship had closed circuit television in her engine room so that the engineer on watch could see every corner of the ship just by the flick of a switch. That and other mechanical devices eliminated the need for 13 men from the engine room compliment. The laundry was located in a centralised area near the bottom of the vessel so that soiled linens could be despatched in chutes rather than on hand trucks. An escalator and elevator between the kitchen and storerooms and the dining room speeded up the delivery of food while reducing the numbers of staff required in the kitchen.

Another advanced aspect of *Sagafjord*'s design was the fact that she was fitted with a bow-thruster to facilitate docking manoeuvres at cruise ports. It is believed that she was the only passenger ship in regular service at that time to be so equipped.

With the naming ceremony complete the sparkling elegant new flagship departed Toulon on 18 September 1965 on her delivery voyage to Oslo, arriving there on the 24th. Later that day she departed on a very special 8-hour cruise for distinguished guests: the most distinguished of these being His Majesty King Olav V. The cruise took her very special passengers down the Oslofjord and briefly out into the North Sea before returning to prepare for her official 'maiden voyage.' *Sagafjord* remained in Oslo for a week, being shown off to the world's shipping press and the travel trade. On Saturday 2 October with blasts from her siren, and bedecked with flags, *Sagafjord* moved away from her berth and headed down the Oslofjord. Her maiden voyage had begun, though with a far from maximum capacity of passengers. She made brief calls at Kristiansand and Copenhagen to embark more passengers before heading towards the Atlantic and New York.

Sagafjord's Master was Captain Odd Aspelund. He had first gone to sea, at the age of 15, as a pantry boy aboard the liner *Stavangerfjord*. After serving some while as a deck hand he spent three years studying at nautical school in Oslo in order to pass the necessary examinations to become a deck officer. By 1954 he had the command of the cargo liner *Trondhjemsfjord* and later returned to *Stavangerfjord* as her Master. Prior to being assigned to *Sagafjord* he had commanded the company's former flagship, *Bergensfjord*.

Sagafjord made a triumphant arrival in New York eight days after leaving Oslo, on 23 October. The New York Herald Tribune reported: "Norwegian America Line's flagship *Sagafjord* made her New York debut yesterday when she arrived on her maiden voyage from Oslo with 482 passengers. The $20 million, 24,000-ton liner received a royal welcome as she glided up the bay. Crown Prince Harald of Norway, in New York on a brief visit, was in the official welcoming party that boarded the ship off Staten Island. After greeting Captain Odd Aspelund, the Prince watched the traditional harbour greetings from the bridge as the new liner made her way to Pier 45, Hudson River on 10th Street." The newspaper went on to report that the ship had been built specifically for cruising out of New York and quoted the Line's general manager, Christian Hendriksen, who had said: "… if she is allowed to operate without being hampered". He was referring to the pending legislation that threatened to regulate cruise operations from American ports. *Sagafjord* remained in New York for three days, during which time she was 'introduced' to the travelling public, being open between 3.30 and 7 p.m., with visitors being asked to donate just $1 for the benefit of the Norwegian Seamen's church in Brooklyn.

On Friday 15 October *Sagafjord* sailed from New York, back to Oslo – again calling at Copenhagen and Kristiansand. On 8 November she was back again in New York and was being made ready for a lengthy series of cruises. The first of these cruises was a 19-day Thanksgiving cruise to the West Indies, this was followed by two further similar cruises, one of 15-days, and a Christmas Holiday cruise of 17 days. On 8 January 1966 she sailed from New York on the kind of cruise that would ultimately make her a legend amongst cruise ships, a 93-day trip around the world,

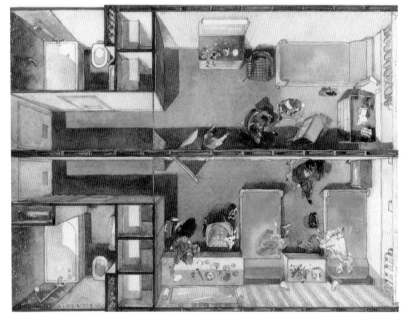

Top: *Sagafjord* alongside at Southampton: every bit as graceful as the previous liners in the fleet.

Bottom: *Sagafjord* had many interconnecting cabins that helped make her ideal for long cruise voyages.

Top: One of *Sagafjord*'s particularly spacious cabins.

Bottom: The indoor pool aboard *Sagafjord*: nearby were a sauna, massage rooms and a gymnasium.

Lido Bar.

calling at 21 ports. This was followed by a 32-day European Spring Blossoms cruise and then on 24 June, in time for her passengers to enjoy the midnight sun, she left on a North Cape and Northern Europe cruise of 45-days' duration. Such lengthy cruises underlined Norwegian America's commitment to the luxury end of the cruise market and as such *Sagafjord* earned an enviable reputation, maintaining the Norwegian America Line reputation of "Carefree Cruises" and upholding the company's motto of "Seamanship and Service in the Norwegian Tradition."

For a brief while Norwegian America Line operated the three liners, *Oslofjord*, *Bergensfjord* and *Sagafjord*. However, by 1969 *Oslofjord* had been placed on a three-year charter to Costa. Encouraged by the success of *Sagafjord* the company had decided that it was time to order a new consort for her. Whilst *Bergensfjord* was only 13-years old she had been built as an Atlantic liner, albeit one with a secondary role as a cruise ship, and while still extremely popular and undeniably luxurious, passenger's tastes and requirements had changed and she was now looking a little dated against the coolly chic and elegant *Sagafjord*. Another factor was of course the dominance of the aircraft across the Atlantic, as a consequence Norwegian America Line, like many other famous companies, continued to phase out their transatlantic service. A new ship of a modern design oriented more towards cruising was what was needed. In 1966 Norwegian America's

greatest rivals, Swedish America Line, had taken delivery of the *Kungsholm* and this superb new liner, along with her near sister vessel *Gripsholm*, was also operating long and luxurious cruises from New York with considerable success. The German Atlantic Line took delivery of their luxurious new liner *Hamburg* in March 1969, she was another ship designed for long-haul cruises of several weeks duration. Elsewhere other radically modern ships were being built for the lower end of the cruise market. However, more significantly for Norwegian America, was the fact that three major Norwegian shipping companies were in the process of forming a new cruise line that would operate three deluxe cruise ships aimed squarely at the market which Norwegian America and Swedish America called their own – the very wealthy of North America. The days of the traditional ocean liner were all but finished but a whole new breed of cruise ships were in the process of being designed and built. It was time for Norwegian America to act, so, on 5 December 1969 they placed an order for a new ship. Once again they turned to Swan, Hunter at Newcastle-upon-Tyne (the builders of *Bergensfjord*) and the vessel was due for delivery in 1973.

In September 1970 *Bergensfjord* was given an extensive refurbishment (including the installation of a permanent outdoor pool). This refurbishment was meant to bring her more in line with *Sagafjord*, and of course to make her a more

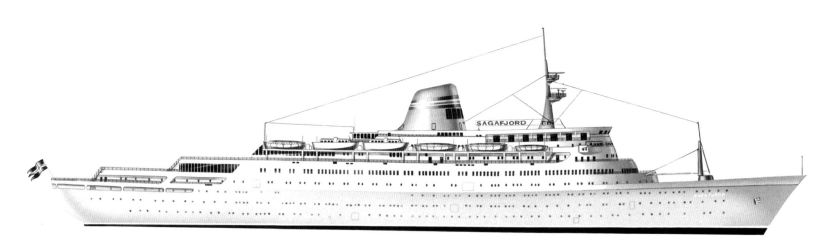

A drawing issued by Norwegian America Line in 1980 showing her new profile.

attractive vessel to a potential purchaser once they had taken delivery of the new ship. These plans however, were short-lived. On 8 January 1971 the French liner *Antilles* struck an uncharted rock off the Caribbean island of Mustique. As a result she ruptured one of her fuel tanks, causing oil to spill out into the boiler room, where it caught fire. Sadly, it was the end for the lovely *Antilles* and she sunk. As French Line had been using the *Antilles* to maintain their regular liner service between France and their Caribbean islands they were very anxious to find a replacement vessel, and quickly. Their search led them to the *Bergensfjord* and so keen were they to buy the ship that they offered Norwegian America a sum greater than they could refuse: even though construction on her replacement had not even begun. The sale was concluded swiftly and in fact by March she was in effect a French ship. However, *Bergensfjord* completed her 1971 cruise programme including one final Atlantic crossing from Oslo during August. Her final cruise under the Norwegian America Line flag was an 18-day cruise to the Mediterranean from Tilbury. Back in the river Thames on 9 October she hoist the Tricolor of France and was renamed *De Grasse*.

Sadly, she would not be a success as *De Grasse*, though it was mainly the rapidly increasing cost of fuel as well as labour costs that hastened her end with French Line: by the end of 1973 she was once again for sale. Several companies were interested in buying her including Home Lines for cruising out of New York, and Israeli

company for use in a static role as both hotel and casino. Instead it was another Norwegian company, Thoresen Ltd, that bought her and in November of that year they took delivery and re-named her *Rasa Sayang*.

Although once again Norwegian owned she was registered in Singapore, and she arrived in that port in January 1974 to begin a programme of 14-day cruises to Indonesia, South Pacific Islands and sometimes up to Hong Kong, Manila and China. It appeared that she was again destined for a successful career as she built up a good reputation with her cruises linked to diverse fly-cruise packages in both America and Europe. For over three years *Rasa Sayang* cruised around the Coral Seas and Indonesia, then on 1 June 1977, while sailing through the Straits of Malacca, a fire broke out in the crew's recreation room. While the fire was confined to the crew's quarters the passengers were evacuated from the ship. Two members of the crew died fighting the fire and three others were reported missing. More damage was done to the ship by the water used to fight the fire than the actual fire itself. Although salvage tugs stood by the ship was still manoeuvrable, and under command of her master, and she arrived back in Singapore on 3 June under her own power.

On 23 June it was announced that *Rasa Sayang* would resume her cruising schedule on 4 July, at the completion of the repair work. As well as damage to the crew quarters some of her passenger cabins had also been affected by both smoke

Designers sketches
of her newly restyled
public rooms:

Main Lounge.

Veranda Café.

Norwegian America Line promoting days at sea.

and water. Only two cruises, one of 14 days and one of 5 days had needed to be cancelled.

Rasa Sayang became the first cruise ship to call at Vietnam since the war there. The call took place in February 1978 but just a few months later, on 3 June, Thoresen announced that the ship would be withdrawn from service – just two weeks later! The announcement came as a surprise as the ship had continued to be very popular and was sailing fully booked on most of her cruises. On 18 June she was placed in lay-up.

It was, in effect, the end for the former *Bergensfjord* even though several plans would be put forward for her further employment. In January 1979, after it had been reported that she had been sold to a Cypriot company, Sunlit Cruises, who planned to re-name her *Golden Moon*, she sailed for the Mediterranean. On her arrival she was again placed in lay-up, along with several other redundant liners and cruise ships. A few months later it was announced that a Dutch company, Nederlands Cruise Maatschappij Bestevaer were to charter the ship from Sunlit Cruises. Their plan, after refitting the ship, was to operate her on a series of cruises out of Rotterdam to Norway, the Baltic and the Mediterranean, under the name *Prins van Oranje*. The cruises were scheduled to begin on 18 May 1979. Sadly, this ambitious plan came to nothing, as in September the ship was still in Piraeus and was reportedly still undergoing repairs. In March 1980, with quite a bit of publicity, a brochure was issued that revealed that the ship would revert to the name *Rasa Sayang* and that she would sail, under charter to CTC Lines. The first brochure issued showed that she would be departing Piraeus on 2 November for Naples, Gibraltar, Tangier, Lisbon and Southampton. Further publicity material announced a voyage to South Africa and Australia: departing Southampton on 13 November and then from Sydney a series of 12 cruises to various South Pacific islands. This was just the beginning: a further announcement was made indicating that the charter would be for 3 years.

On 27 August, while undergoing repairs at Perama, a fire broke out in her engine room. The local fire brigade were unable to stop it from spreading, and soon the fire engulfed the whole ship. She was towed out to Kynosura where the burnt out wreck of the once beautiful *Bergensfjord* sank, a total loss.

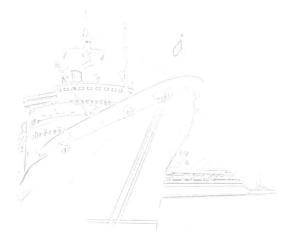

CHAPTER FOUR

Vistafjord

The insurance that was paid as a result of the loss of the *Oslofjord* (when sailing as *Fulvia* for Costa Line in July 1970) and the money received from French Line for the *Bergensfjord* put Norwegian America Line in a good financial position when the $35 million new flagship was ready to be launched in 1972 from the Neptune yard of Swan Hunter Shipbuilders Ltd.

While the early 1970s may have been ushering in a whole new age of passenger shipping, with strikingly designed vessels that bore little or no relationship to their predecessors, the directors of Norwegian America Line and their technical design team, once again lead by Kaare Haug, were largely influenced by the ships of their recent past. It was announced that she would be named *Vistafjord*. A new name for the company, and yet it evoked all the traditions of the Line. Indeed, this was a very clever move as the lines of the ship were a beautiful combination of both the traditional and the modern. In many respects she would have a profile similar to that of *Sagafjord*, she would, however, be one deck higher and have a taller and slightly more angular funnel. The lines of *Sagafjord* were graceful, fluid and sweeping, while there would be something a little more stiff and angular about *Vistafjord*. She was, nevertheless, still a most handsome ship, and even before she was launched, when Norwegian America Line issued a photograph of a model of how the ship would look, her design was regarded as being almost anachronistic, especially when compared to the striking design of the ships being built for Royal Viking Line.

On 15 May 1972 *Vistafjord* was launched. Work on the ship progressed quickly and just under 11 months later, between 6 and 9 April 1973, she ran her trials. Trials were a most appropriate word as there was a gale raging for most of this time. Despite this she was still able to make over 20 knots and Kaare Haug was quoted as saying that: "she behaved like a Swan." There is no doubt this was true, as *Vistafjord* has proved herself to be a good sea-boat but nevertheless it still seems like a bad pun! On 15 May, exactly one year after she was launched, *Vistafjord* was delivered to Norwegian America Line – four months ahead of schedule. As a gesture of gratitude to the workers that had been involved in the construction of

the ship Norwegian America awarded them a cash bonus. This generous gesture unfortunately backfired, as those remaining workers at the shipyard, who had not been part of the *Vistafjord's* construction, went on strike for not having been included in the award!

On 15 May 1973, after the naming ceremony, which was performed by Mrs Agnes Henriksen, wife of the Managing Director of Norwegian America Line, *Vistafjord* sailed from Newcastle-upon-Tyne for Norway. She first called at Stavanger, and the on 17 May – Norway's Independence Day – she arrived to an enthusiastic reception in Oslo. It was by one of those most delightful of coincidences that *Bergensfjord* was also in Oslo on that day –the oldest and the newest liners of the fleet and both products of Swan, Hunter.

Vistafjord had the same hull form and dimensions as *Sagafjord* and her machinery arrangement was also very similar. Her superstructure was a modern interpretation of the lines of a classic passenger liner. Again, as in *Sagafjord*, aluminium played a considerable part in the construction of the new ship, with over 600 tons of it being used for the whole of the deckhouse structure. Experience with both *Bergensfjord* and *Sagafjord* had shown that aluminium superstructure had shown that it required very little maintenance and the aluminium-to-steel joints had given no trouble. An elaborate system of neoprene sheets, stainless steel bolts and zinc-plated pins were used to join the aluminium structure to the steel hull of the ship. Because of the excellent stability conditions of the *Sagafjord*, Norwegian America decided that the superstructure of the new ship could be extended both fore and aft, and that an extra deck could be added. This meant that *Vistafjord's* passenger capacity was increased by 100 over that of the *Sagafjord*, and the amount of public space was increased substantially. Also, to improve passenger space in way of the public rooms and open deck spaces, the deckhouse was almost one metre wider than the hull. Since the hull form of *Vistafjord* followed that of *Sagafjord* no tank model tests were carried out. Given that *Vistafjord* would have a larger superstructure this does seem a little surprising. The possibility of including a bulbous forefoot at the bow was investigated but on balance, it was

Although entering service in 1973 *Vistafjord* had all the grace of a liner of an earlier generation.

decided that the excellent sea-kindliness of *Sagafjord* outweighed the possibility of obtaining an additional ½ knot in the speed with the bulbous bow fitted.

Vistafjord had nine decks: Officers, Sun, Promenade, Verandah, Upper, Main, A, B and C Decks. The passenger cabins were arranged on five of them, with the majority being on Main and A Decks. Eighty per cent of them being outside cabins and there were a considerable number of single cabins. On the Promenade and Sun Decks a number of the cabins were arranged as suites. The joinery department of Swan Hunter were responsible for the cabin furniture throughout the ship though there was in fact very little actual woodwork employed. Since the ship was constructed to Method 1 standards, with regard to fire containment, some

850,000 sq. ft of Marinite panels were employed throughout the ship for corridor and inter-cabin bulkheads, linings, ceilings and doors. These panels were then veneered with the appropriate laminates.

The forward staircase was in the form of an oval and was very similar to the one aboard *Sagafjord*. With the exception of the main dining room, all the principal public rooms were situated on Verandah Deck and were laid out along largely similar arrangement to those of *Sagafjord*. Kay Korbing, the Copenhagen-based designer was responsible for the designs of the public rooms. Forward there was the almost circular Garden Lounge and aft on the starboard side was the smaller Norse Lounge and Club 52, the card room. Much use of light veneers had been

Vistafjord dressed overall in flags.

used in the decoration of these rooms. Opposite, on the port side was the North Cape Bar, this was decorated in various shades of blue, with a dramatic group of orange chairs and settees arranged by the aft, dark blue, wall. Aft of this was a writing room and library. Filling the space between the bar and the Norse Lounge was the cinema. Just aft of amidships was the 8,500 sq. ft Grand Ballroom. All 550 passengers could be accommodated in the room, which had an elegant decorative scheme of yellow, light olive green and deep orange. Only four small pillars were located in this very large room, which had a maximum height of 15ft, and this was achieved by the use of large aluminium box-girders hidden in the ceiling above. This spectacular and spacious room was further complimented at night by the swimming pool aft, which could be turned into a coloured fountain. A small nightclub, Club Viking, was at the after end of Promenade Deck. The main decorative colour was red and there was a small, oval-shaped metal dance floor with a gold glitter finish. In order to allow passengers ample flexibility in their seating requirements, the dining room had a capacity for 620. Designed by Njal Eide, the very large room was well lit by full-length windows on each side, allowing the room to live up to its name: the Vista Dining Room. Tables, with orange linen, were arranged for two, four or six, the chairs being either orange or off-white leatherette to match the orange and red patterned carpet. Communication with the galley, on the deck below, was by two escalators. These were located in the

Top: *Vistafjord* at Nassau, the funnel of the Italian liner *Leonardo Da Vinci* can be glimpsed behind her.

Bottom: Looking rather larger than her 24,000 tons, *Vistafjord* at La Corunna.

Above, both pictures: In the early years of her career *Vistafjord* was a regular sight in the river Thames, with many of her cruises departing from Tilbury.

Top: Elegance 1970s style, *Vistafjord*'s Dining Room.

Bottom: The Norse Lounge.

Top: The Club Viking.

Bottom: *Vistafjord*'s Ballroom was particularly elegant.

centre of the room behind a partition, the after part of which was covered in a dramatic brass sculpture. As with *Sagafjord, Vistafjord* was decorated with a significant number of outstanding pieces of modern decorative art by noted Danish and Norwegian artists. The well decorated rooms had an easy appeal on the eye – nowhere was there any sign of the type of garish décor that was becoming popular aboard other new cruise ships.

In their report on the ship the journal *The Motor Ship* stated: "...the ship is a credit to its builders who have shown that passenger ship building in the UK is not dead."

On 22 May 1973 *Vistafjord* departed Oslo on her maiden voyage to New York, arriving there on 31 May., having also called at Kristiansand and Copenhagen. It was to be one of just a mere handful of scheduled transatlantic voyages back and forth between Oslo and New York. *Vistafjord* had been built for cruising in the grand manner, long luxurious voyages of several weeks duration. Her space and elegance quickly ensured her a place amongst the world's elite of luxury liners, rapidly acquiring her Five Star status. Her cruises during the remainder of 1973 were as lengthy as they were diverse: in August and early September she cruised to Scandinavia and into the Baltic, having arrived back in New York on

10 September she departed the following day for a 42-day Mediterranean sojourn. She then headed for South America and into the Pacific as far as Easter Island. During this 55-day excursion she called at 17ports. This cruise however, was far from a success for Norwegian America as there were just 180 passengers on board. Following a Caribbean Christmas cruise she departed on 4 January 1974 on a 94-day, 23-port, cruise around the world. On her return she sailed on a 40-day cruise to the Mediterranean and the Greek Islands. This was followed by a 42-day North Cape cruise, a 30-day cruise to the Baltic and a further month cruising the Mediterranean.

During those months of 1974 *Sagafjord* had been employed on very similar itineraries. On 28 January she had sailed from New York on a 73-day South Pacific cruise. Then after a mere 14 days cruising the Caribbean she had departed for a 35-day European cruise, this was followed by a 32-day North Cape cruise. *Sagafjord* also undertook two cruises from Copenhagen, one to the North Cape and one into the Baltic. During the later months of 1974 both *Sagafjord* and *Vistafjord* undertook Caribbean cruises of 10, 12 or 14-days, and to some extent this was an indication of things to come.

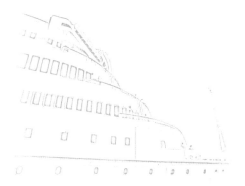

CHAPTER FIVE

The sisters together

The cruise market was undergoing changes and there was a certain trend away from the type of long cruises that ships like *Sagafjord* and *Vistafjord* had been designed for; shorter cruises and fly-cruises were becoming more fashionable, and more desirable: the small number of passengers that had been attracted to *Vistafjord*'s 55-day cruise around South America being a very clear indication of that. Also, the fact that just five months after *Vistafjord*'s entry into service saw the fuel crisis, with the cost of all kinds of fuel increasing enormously did not help.

Vistafjord begun 1975 with a 79-day 'Four Continents' cruise and this was followed by a 39-day cruise in the Mediterranean. That was, however, the end of *Vistafjord*'s time as a New York-based cruise ship, Norwegian America had decided to position her in Europe and on 21 May she sailed across the Atlantic to operate a whole new series of cruises. She would sail from Southampton and Tilbury, and from Hamburg while *Sagafjord* would remain operating out of New York. Norwegian America Line wanted in effect to take some of the market that was more usually attracted to the German cruise ship, *Europa*. It was in 1975 that their greatest rivals in that very special niche of the luxury cruise market, Swedish America Line, had ceased operations due to the high costs associated with operating ships registered in Sweden and with fully unionised Swedish crews. Thus, the flawless *Gripsholm* had been sold in 1974 to a Greek operator Karageorgis Line. The beautiful *Kungsholm* had sailed in solitary splendour for a short while before being sold to Flagship Cruises. It was to be a short-lived career as before long she was sold again to P&O. However, *Sagafjord* was faced with new competition, in the form of the Royal Viking Line. Dramatically styled compared to the traditional elegance of *Sagafjord* (and *Vistafjord*, which was built at the same time as the Royal Viking ships) they were aiming at exactly the same market, and with three virtually identical ships each offering the very best of service, they were soon able to capture a large slice of it. With three ships they were also able to offer a greater diversity of cruises, from a mere 4 or 7 days coastal cruising to 30-plus days to Europe or 66 days cruising the South Pacific. Whilst the sleekly new Royal Viking

trio lured many passengers, *Sagafjord* in her ten years of service, had developed a very loyal following and she therefore continued to sail at full capacity – albeit of only 450 passengers – but it was her air of spaciousness that was one of her greatest luxuries.

Despite the fact that *Vistafjord* was proving popular in Europe Norwegian America Line was nevertheless facing the problem of their fixed operational costs being spread over their two-ship fleet, ships of limited capacity. In 1976 the company realised that drastic action would have to be taken if they were to survive. Their reputation was built on its uncompromising quality of service and such a reputation made economy measures very difficult. Even when fully booked *Sagafjord* had begun to lose money and the directors of Norwegian America considered the drastic action of selling her. Karageorgis Lines, which was successfully operating the former *Gripsholm* as the *Navarino* in the Mediterranean, were looking to expand their cruising operations and *Sagafjord* was considered to be a potentially admirable fleet mate. Negotiations between the two companies took place but for reasons unknown no sale was concluded. So after *Sagafjord* had completed a long Mediterranean cruise, on 15 October 1976 she was laid up while a decision was made regarding her future. The options were simple, either sell the ship or expand her passenger capacity. Fortunately, Norwegian America could see the good sense in retaining this very popular ship (also, being the operators of just a single ship could well have increased their problems rather than solved them). Therefore it was decided to increase the number of passengers that *Sagafjord* could accommodate and twenty-five of her large single cabins were made into doubles. She returned to service in April 1977, with an Easter cruise to the Caribbean. This was followed by a full programme, of just five long cruises from New York to the Mediterranean, the North Cape and Norwegian fjords, Ireland and the British Isles, that took her through until early October. They were promoted as "Deluxe European Cruise Holidays – a touch of yesterday today."

With the harsh realities of the present day impinging upon the rarefied atmosphere aboard the Norwegian America sisters further economies had to be made.

Norwegian America Line passengers spoiled for choice – which of the lovely sisters to choose?

Vistafjord – dramatic by night.

Vistafjord had been built with 17 inside cabins down on C Deck. However, it appears that initially these were not used for accommodating passengers, even though they were designed as passenger cabins. In the winter of 1976, during a refit, these cabins were brought into passenger use while some single cabins were converted into doubles thereby increasing her passenger capacity to 700. With the great popularity of the 'fly-cruise' concept Norwegian America abandoned any ideas of sending *Vistafjord* on a long and exotic winter cruise. Instead, she spent the winter of 1976/77 in the Caribbean mostly on two alternating 17-day itineraries, sailing out of Port Everglades. Between June and early September she operated a series of Scandinavian and Northern Europe cruises, embarking passengers at both Tilbury and Hamburg: *Vistafjord* had begun to establish a very loyal passenger base in Germany. The early autumn was spent cruising the Mediterranean and Black Sea. Following on from the success of the previous winter's Caribbean programme, this was repeated over the winter months of 1977/78.

Sagafjord was returned to Europe briefly during 1978 to operate a series of 14-day cruises to Mediterranean ports from Genoa, between April and June. She then returned to New York and continued her more usual long summer cruises to Scandinavia. The employment of *Vistafjord* during the winter of 1978 was to be somewhat different to that of the previous two years. Instead, on 29 October she sailed from Genoa on a 41-day cruise to the islands of the Indian Ocean and the exotic ports of East Africa. Her Christmas and New Year cruise departed Southampton for the Canary Islands and Dakar, and it was not until 7 January 1979 that she sailed from Southampton for the Caribbean. *Sagafjord* had been maintaining the role of Caribbean cruise ship but on *Vistafjord*'s arrival in Port Everglades on 20 January she resumed this role, while *Sagafjord* set off on another cruise around the world.

Sweeping curves and graceful lines...

...two perfect liners.

Vistafjord returned to Europe in April, initially to the Mediterranean and then to Scandinavia for the midsummer months. On her return from the world cruise, *Sagafjord* resumed her usual employment of long cruises to Europe. They would be the last of her cruises in the grand manner. Her 13 May 1979 departure was an unusual one in that she sailed from Port Everglades, rather than New York, on a 41-day cruise to the Mediterranean. Whilst this cruise ended back in Port Everglades, she then continued on up to New York before again crossing the Atlantic, this time to Scotland, Norway, the Baltic, London and the Channel Islands. This was followed by a 38-day cruise to Southern Norway and the Baltic capitals. On 14 September *Sagafjord* departed New York on a 44-day Eastern Mediterranean cruise, it was to be Norwegian America's last long European cruise from that port. What had become established as a cruising tradition had come to an end. She spent the final months of the year cruising the Caribbean from Port Everglades before embarking again on another world cruise. Having spent the late summer months in the Mediterranean, *Vistafjord* then crossed the Atlantic to Barbados from where she cruised down along the Brazilian coast as far as Santos. Back to Barbados she then spent the winter in the Caribbean.

While both the ships had been sailing on this diverse array of cruises the directors of Norwegian America in Oslo had continued to look for ways to make them more profitable and they felt that they had found the ideal solution. Instead of competing against their rivals Royal Viking Line, who were after all another Norwegian company, why not merge operations? On 10 December 1979 Norwegian America Line made the announcement that the two companies would merge. In fact as from 1 January 1980 Norwegian America would cease to exist: *Sagafjord* and *Vistafjord* would be repainted in Royal Viking Line livery and would be renamed, *Royal Viking Saga* and *Royal Viking Vista* – the changes would be in place by 1981. Thus, it was in effect a takeover rather than a merger and these moves were given stockholder approval at a meeting held on 21 December. Best-laid plans however, do not always go as one expects. The two companies could not agree on the future of

Vistafjord's forward superstructure.

Senior officers on the Bridge wing of *Vistafjord* as she sails from Tilbury.

Take Your Ship to the Caribbean

Carrying only 635 passengers *Vistafjord* offered the luxury of space.

Sagafjord, quite simply Royal Viking Line did not want the 15-year-old liner to be a part of the new-look fleet. The merger plans were deferred indefinitely. Instead, Leif Hoegh & Co increased their share in the ships from forty to fifty per cent and a new independent company, Norwegian American Cruises, was established on 1 May 1980. Apart from adopting a new company logo, 'NAC', it was business but not as usual. *Sagafjord* was repositioned to Genoa from where she spent the summer on a series of 14-day cruises alternating between the Eastern Mediterranean and the Black Sea. *Vistafjord* operated in a similar pattern between the Baltic and the Norwegian fjords and Spitzbergen.

Having stated that it would continue to look for a partner for its cruise operations NAC, looking to the future, invested considerably in both the ships. On 19 October 1980 *Sagafjord* arrived at the Hamburg yard of Blohm & Voss for an extensive refit and refurbishment. The work, which would cost $24 million

resulted in a striking new profile for the ship: a look that was not greeted with wholehearted praise. A whole new deck, of what were described as 'super suites' each with its own private balcony, had been built above the bridge and forward of the funnel. This new structure slanted forward, and while giving the ship a similar profile to *Vistafjord*, it rather lessened the elegance of her otherwise gracefully curved and swept back superstructure. Njal Eide and Arnstein Arnberg, both of whom had a long association with the decoration of Norwegian America ships, were responsible for the updating of *Sagafjord*'s interiors. The most significant feature of this updating was the changes made to the Grand Ballroom. The simple and elegant decorative scheme was replaced, the new one being totally the opposite: mainly in shades of orange and red. Curious glass-fibre curved shapes covered the upper parts of her windows that made the outer edges of the room resemble the interior of an aircraft. What had once been the children's room and

A late afternoon departure from Tilbury.

latterly the Dance Studio, just aft of the North Cape Bar was turned into a casino. Four more cabins were constructed on what had been known as Sun Deck in the space that had been the galley serving the Club Polaris when it had operated as the First Class Dining Room. The ship was fitted with a new air-conditioning system and new auxiliary machinery and she was now listed as having accommodation for 505 passengers. On 18 December 1980 the new-look *Sagafjord* sailed from Hamburg for Port Everglades to embark passengers for another cruise around the world. While *Sagafjord* had been refitting *Vistafjord* had sailed from Genoa on an exotic 41-day cruise calling at ports in the Red Sea, East Africa, various islands in the Indian Ocean and India.

While *Sagafjord* had still been refitting the last remnants of Norwegian America Line came to an end with the sale of their shares in NAC to Leif Hoegh

& Co. for $20.3 million. On her return from the Indian Ocean, *Vistafjord* also underwent some refitting and refurbishment work, though to a far lesser extent than her sister. Her former card room was transformed into a casino and the C Deck cabins were no longer classified as passenger accommodation.

Despite the changes, both *Sagafjord* and *Vistafjord* were largely the same as they had been when operated by Norwegian America Line, they still carried the same yellow funnels with the red white and blue bands, the service aboard was still flawless, they were still regarded as being amongst the very best cruise ships in the world, and for *Sagafjord* this was quite an accolade as she was now over 15 years old. (It is interesting in fact to note that Antoinette Deland, apparently an authority on cruise ships and the editor of *Fielding's Worldwide Guide to Cruising*, stated in one issue of the guide that was published shortly after the refit of *Sagafjord*: "*Sagafjord* is a great lady of the sea – some say without equal. While her physical beauty is certainly surpassed by the Royal Viking fleet, there is a special quality of contentment aboard this cruise ship.") Even with the additional deck of balcony cabins there were those that would certainly question Miss Deland's comparison of *Sagafjord* and the ships of Royal Viking Line. However, while *Sagafjord* and *Vistafjord* still presented a familiar image their new owner introduced entirely new itineraries. Not only would *Sagafjord* sail from New York and Port Everglades, now she would also operate from San Francisco. Her new itineraries included cruises to New England and Canada and up to Alaska. In July 1981 NAC announced their withdrawal from the Caribbean stating: "it is not right for our size ships and our clientele." Instead, *Vistafjord* returned to the Indian Ocean, making two long cruises to East Africa and India during the winter of 1982-83. The ships were both being marketed well and it was paying off with a good level of passenger bookings. NAC let it be known that they were considering the possibility of a third ship. Despite this, however, there were rumours that both the ships were available for sale.

Vistafjord in the Kiel Canal.

Vistafjord's dining room staff.

Vistafjord's North Cape Bar.

In home waters: *Vistafjord* at Stavanger.

Sagafjord at Hammerfest early in her career, before the additions to her superstructure.

On 11 May 1983 it was announced by Trafalgar House that their subsidiary company, Cunard Steamship Co Plc, had bought both *Sagafjord* and *Vistafjord* from Leif Hoegh & Co. AS of Oslo for £47 million. The ships were to be delivered to Cunard five months later, in October. It was also announced that they would transfer from Norwegian to Bahamian registry. The purchase of course brought to an end the rumours that had circulated regarding the future of the two ships and had also ended the protracted speculation that Cunard were planning to build new ships to supplement the cruise programmes then operated by the *Queen Elizabeth 2* and the *Cunard Countess* and *Cunard Princess*. While there were reports that implied Cunard were considering renaming the ships *Cunard Saga* and *Cunard Vista* this appears to have been just a rumour. The suggestion of the adoption of these names was, however, an indication of the way in which Cunard was expected (by some people) to operate the ships – as companion vessels to the more mass-market *Countess* and *Princess*. It had been a long time since the Cunard Line had been associated with the segment of the cruise market that *Sagafjord* and *Vistafjord* represented and therefore there were a lot of misconceptions about Cunard's plans for the ships.

Their final cruises for Norwegian America Cruises were journeys of nostalgia. On 13 August 1983 *Vistafjord* sailed from Hamburg on a 14-day Scandinavian and Baltic cruise. It was her final cruise, as a Norwegian ship, in those very familiar waters. On her arrival in Oslo, on 25 August, a nostalgic home-coming, she was visited by her past Norwegian America Line captains, including her first, Captain Roald Halvorsen. *Vistafjord* then sailed for Genoa to operate a series of four cruises in the Eastern Mediterranean; her very last under the Norwegian flag departing on 9 October.

CHAPTER SIX

The Cunard years

On their passing into Cunard Line ownership *Sagafjord* and *Vistafjord* were both given $15 million refits. The work on *Vistafjord* being carried out in the Malta Drydock's shipyard during December 1983. Her Promenade Deck superstructure was extended aft and involved the removal of the lovely Club Viking altogether, as well as the Sports deck. Fifteen new cabins were constructed in their place, and two other cabins were created just forward of this. The Sun Deck above was also extended and this allowed for the creation of seven cabins. Aft of these cabins was the Club Viking Gallery, which was connected to the newly created Club Viking on the deck below. *Sagafjord*, meanwhile, was drydocked in San Francisco for similar rebuilding work. Her Club Polaris and sports deck were also removed and cabins and a new nightclub built in their place. The Terrace Sun Deck was also extended, but due to the shape of the ship, rather awkwardly. The extension being rather curiously named Officers Deck, except that this contained eleven new passenger cabins and the upper level of the new Club Polaris, rather than accommodation for the officers. On Main Deck her dining room was enlarged by extending it forward either side of the funnel casing: this involved the removal of five passenger cabins. However, the most dramatic change to this room was the creation of windows. Although not particularly low down in her hull *Sagafjord*'s dining room had been built on the very traditional lines of a totally enclosed room, without any natural light. The cutting of windows into her hull gave the room a similar feel to the dining room aboard *Vistafjord*. While the extending of the decks aft, on both ships, in order to create more revenue earning passenger cabins was obviously essential the new structures somewhat compromised their otherwise graceful lines. While their funnels were painted in the traditional Cunard red and black both ships retained their names. Cunard had not only bought the ships but they had also bought the goodwill of Norwegian America Cruises and the right to use that name and the names of the ships.

While the passenger capacity on each ship had been increased there was in fact no intention of turning them to the same market as the *Cunard Countess* and *Cunard Princess*. *Sagafjord* and *Vistafjord* were still to be catering to the very upper end of the cruise market. In fact at a Press Conference held shortly before the ships went to be rebuilt, when the plans for the ships were announced to the public, the company president, Ralph Bahna, made repeated references to the long-departed *Caronia* – the ship that perhaps more than any other represented the very epitome of deluxe cruising. Both *Sagafjord* and *Vistafjord* were to take on that illustrious mantle. However, whilst *Caronia* had been renowned for her lengthy cruises Cunard intended to employ *Sagafjord* and *Vistafjord* on very similar cruises to those they had recently been operating for Norwegian America Cruises. Cunard had not bought the goodwill of NAC for nothing, they had every intention of retaining those passengers already loyal to the two ships and having modernised the ships, intended to attract new passengers to these classic beauties. Indeed, the ships were even marketed differently to the rest of the Cunard fleet, under the Cunard/NAC banner and those passengers who were already familiar with the ships had the pleasure of finding that many of the crew members had elected to remain with the ships.

Back in 1983 *Vistafjord* had, to a certain extent, become a movie star. A film crew, along with various actors, including Jon Voight, were aboard her during a Mediterranean cruise the previous year filming scenes for the movie, 'Table for Five'. The ship remained more memorable than the poorly received film! While the television series 'Love Boat' is firmly associated with the *Pacific* and *Island Princess* vessels, during May 1985 a double episode of the series was shot aboard *Vistafjord*. Several famous 'Hollywood names' were on board for the filming among them were Cesar Romero and Lorenzo Lamas. The two episodes were shown on American television the following May.

Sagafjord remained the American-based ship: often operating summertime cruises up to Alaska and in the Autumn months across to the Orient for cruises between Hong Kong and Kobe, calling at ports in China and South Korea. During the winter she would depart on the type of cruise for which she had become so well known: perhaps three months around the Pacific and Orient, or even right around the world. *Vistafjord* was based in Europe as before, continuing to find

Vistafjord at Corfu. Note the additions to her aft superstructure.

The perfect image of a cruise: *Sagafjord* at anchor. Note her aft superstructure also extended.

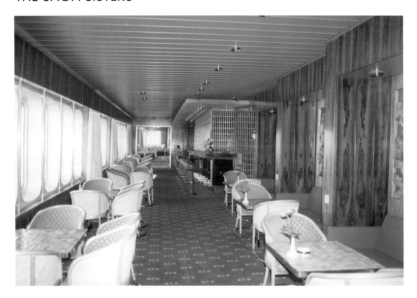

Sagafjord's North Cape Bar...

...and Card Room.

great popularity with German as well as British passengers. She was mainly based in Hamburg during the early summer for cruises to Scandinavia and the Baltic, repositioning to Genoa for Mediterranean cruises. During the winter she would cross the Atlantic to Port Everglades for cruises to the Caribbean and beyond.

Although this was largely the regular pattern of employment for the ships there were of course variations to it. Briefly, during 1986 while the *Queen Elizabeth 2* was being re-engined, *Sagafjord* resumed her original role and undertook some transatlantic voyages. During the remaining years of the 1980's *Sagafjord* regained all the lustre that had begun to falter during those uncertain days of Norwegian America Cruises. Despite her age she was the highest-rated cruise ship, with a five-star plus rating. The trio of Royal Viking Line having by this time been lengthened and with their passenger capacity increased to 700 had been reduced to a mere five star rating. *Sagafjord* was regarded as being the equal to the former *Kungsholm*. During her world cruises her passenger capacity would be held at its former level of approximately 450. While many passengers returned to the ship year after year for the long winter cruise there were other passengers who regarded the ship almost as their home, one lady staying aboard for four years, whilst another when ever she boarded the ship, filled a suite with her own furniture.

Vistafjord never quite managed to attain that extra 'plus' marking to her five star rating but was nevertheless regarded as a most elegant cruise ship. Being a very European ship her American passengers did not always feel quite as comfortable as they would have liked with her mix of German and British passengers. It also seems that it was difficult to comfortably accommodate all of her passengers, if she was sailing at her increased capacity, in her dining room.

On 5 January 1987 *Vistafjord* sailed from Los Angeles on a most unusual cruise, an 80-day 'America's Cup Odyssey'. The cruise called at several South Pacific islands before making her very first arrival in Sydney, on 25 January. On 2 February she arrived off Fremantle, as the third race of the final series of the America's Cup yacht races was taking place. She remained in port for three days before sailing up to Bali, Singapore, Hong Kong and the rest of her cruise around the Pacific.

Vistafjord begun 1989 with a cruise to the Hawaiian Islands before a transit of the Panama Canal for a series of Caribbean cruises. She then cruised the Amazon up as far as Manaus. In April she sailed from Fort Lauderdale on a 40-day cruise to the Mediterranean and the Black Sea, this 27-port cruise ended in Southampton. After a two week Mediterranean cruise *Vistafjord* then took on the role, albeit briefly, as a transatlantic liner, operating a round-trip voyage, Southampton - New York - Southampton. She was in fact replacing the *Queen Elizabeth 2*, which at the time was returning from a lengthy Japanese charter. The rest of that summer was spent cruising Northern Europe, the Baltic and Norway. By September she was positioned in Genoa for cruises in the Mediterranean and out to the Atlantic islands. By November she was again in the Caribbean. While it was a fairly typical

pattern of employment for her *Sagafjord* had not sailed on quite such a variety of routes during that year. On 17 April she had returned to Fort Lauderdale at the end of her World Cruise. She then undertook three 11 and 12- day 'Bermuda and the Colonial South' cruises. Between 10 June and 4 September she sailed on a series of Alaska cruises; 13 days northwards from Vancouver to Anchorage, and then 12 days calling at the same ports heading south back to Vancouver. During October she made three further cruises to Bermuda, two included calls in New England and one again called at Charleston and Savannah. During November *Sagafjord* cruised up the Amazon and then December was spent cruising the Caribbean.

Thus by the late 1980s *Sagafjord* and *Vistafjord* were firmly established in the Cunard fleet, making them an unbeatable pair for true luxury at sea in the traditional style. By 1990 Cunard had dropped the NAC label in their marketing of the two ships. When they had acquired the *Royal Viking Sun*, in 1994, the three ships, *Sagafjord*, *Vistafjord* and *Royal Viking Sun*, along with the *Sea Goddess I* and *Sea Goddess II* were being marketed under the Cunard – Royal Viking banner. This, however, was short-lived. The company were facing difficulties and the glory days of *Sagafjord* and *Vistafjord* as Cunard cruise ships seemed to be on the wane. Although *Vistafjord* had undergone an extensive refit, two scheduled refits planned for *Sagafjord* had been cancelled and in some circles her future in the Cunard fleet was beginning to be questioned. Cunard's parent company, Trafalgar House, announced at the end of 1995 that they would spend £31 million in restructuring the Line in an attempt to return it to profit. They had suffered an operational loss of £16 million in the year to the end of September 1995. There were rumours that they would divest themselves of Cunard Line altogether in order to

Above left: *Sagafjord* at speed, photographed from on board *Vistafjord*.

Above and overleaf: *Vistafjord*'s remodelled public rooms: the Polaris Club.

Left: *Vistafjord*'s Lido Café.

Left below: Garden Lounge.

Below: Ballroom.

concentrate on their core industries, which were focussed on engineering and off-shore industries. Trafalgar House however, ruled out any possibility of an early sale of the Line stating that the changes would include a restructuring of both management and marketing to capitalise on Cunard's luxury image. The plans were expected to take two years to fully come into effect and Trafalgar House did not expect Cunard to be able to return to profit until some time after the changes had been implemented. City analysts and shipping industry watchers warned that Trafalgar House faced a huge task in re-launching Cunard, stating that the Line had been grossly under-invested, and in the last decade the company had been at a near standstill.

The re-structuring announcement was followed, on 19 December 1995, by the shocking news that *Sagafjord* would be withdrawn from service the following September. It was stated that she was not generating the right returns in her world wide trading mode and that she could not continue trading in this way for much longer. This move was seen as the first to be put in hand to reverse Cunard's losses. Cunard said that they were reviewing a number of options for the ship, including private charters and they also admitted that she could be sold.

Under this cloud of uncertainty *Sagafjord* sailed from Ft Lauderdale on 4 January 1996 on her regular world cruise. Amongst her passengers were one hundred who had been booked to sail on the first world cruise planned for Regency Cruises, to have been operated by their flagship *Regent Sea*: a fact that would have particular poignancy several months later. *Sagafjord* was due to return on 13 April, when after a refit she

Sagafjord at...

...Hamilton, Bermuda.

Alongside at Southampton, *Vistafjord* prepares to depart on another cruise.

Even the Cunard colours could not hide the lines that marked where the Norwegian America Line colours were painted.

would operate some cruises from Ft Lauderdale before sailing for her final season of Alaska cruises. This was not however, the way that things would turn out.

At approximately 10 a.m. on 26 February a generator fire crippled *Sagafjord* while she was in the South China Seas en route from Hong Kong to Kota Kinabalu. Salvage tugs had to be sent from Manila to help get the liner to the Philippines. It was evident that the damage was such that it had hastened the end of *Sagafjord's* career as a part of the Cunard fleet. She arrived in Subic Bay at 2 a.m. on 1 March and shortly afterwards Cunard confirmed the rumours that *Sagafjord* would be withdrawn immediately and that her scheduled cruises for 1996 had been cancelled. Those passengers who wished to continue their cruise were transferred to either the *Royal Viking Sun* or the *Queen Elizabeth 2*, both of which were also sailing on world cruise itineraries. In mid-April, having undergone some repairs, *Sagafjord* was involved in another drama. While she was on her way to the Sembawang shipyard at Singapore for completion of her repair work she went to the aid of a sinking Turkish cargo vessel and rescued 26 members of its crew. *Sagafjord* remained at the Sembawang yard until June.

Meanwhile, back in Britain Cunard was making headline news with the Norwegian engineering and shipbuilding company, Kvaerner, announcing they were going to make a £1 billion bid for Trafalgar House. There was considerable media speculation over what would become of Cunard, the Line suddenly seeming to acquire the status of a "national treasure". While it seemed unlikely that any of the major players in the cruise industry would be interested in the very obvi-

While the penthouse suites may have enhanced *Vistafjord*'s accommodation the addition of the 'go-faster' stripe was unnecessary.

ously ailing company there were nevertheless hysterical press reports of it being sold to Disney. While the P&O chairman had said that he would be prepared to look at Cunard, "at a price," on 4 March Kvaerner made a £904 million agreed takeover bid for Trafalgar House, and they announced that while Cunard was not a part of their long-term plan, selling the Line was not necessarily imminent. It was believed that Kvaerner would probably wait until Cunard showed some financial improvement before selling it.

Just to round off this winter of turmoil and uncertainty, on 4 April the *Royal Viking Sun* ripped her hull and damaged one of her stabilisers after hitting a coral reef in the Red Sea, which resulted in her engine room and generator room being flooded. Those passengers who had transferred to her from *Sagafjord* must have thought they were cursed!

On 21 May it was confirmed that Transocean Tours of Bremen would charter *Sagafjord* for 9 months, the charter to take effect from 15 July 1996. In a curious twist, she would be renamed *Gripsholm*, the name of her former Swedish America Line rival. This had come about because Transocean had hoped to charter the *Regent Sea* (formerly the *Gripsholm*) from Regency Cruises following her world cruise, and they had intended to restore her original name and had begun marketing their forthcoming programme of cruises in this way. Sadly, these plans went seriously awry after the collapse of Regency Cruises in October 1995 with *Regent Sea* tied up in a complex tangle of mortgages and debt – and in fact she was never to sail again. *Sagafjord*, being of very similar size and style to *Regent Sea* therefore appeared to be the ideal replacement to undertake the already announced, and heavily booked, cruise programme. Under the terms of the charter Cunard would continue to operate the deck and engine departments with Transocean being responsible for the hotel operations. At the time the charter was announced it was already being speculated that if the ship performed well Transocean would extend the charter. So it seemed that fate was once again smiling on *Sagafjord*.

Sagafjord arrived in Bremerhaven on 12 July to take up this new phase in her career. Beautiful though *Sagafjord* is, she looked distinctly awkward in her new

Vistafjord berthed with *Crystal Harmony* at Honolulu.

Vistafjord at Greenwich. This was the first and only time that she came that far up the Thames and was anchored there for the 150 years anniversary celebrations of the Cunard Line.

Sagafjord departs Cape Town during a World Cruise.

livery. Her grey hull was adorned with a broad two-tone blue stripe, and her funnel was painted white with a blue top and with the Transocean logo in blue on the sides. Even the name, *Gripsholm*, spelled out in heavy blue lettering above her balconied cabins appeared clumsy.

On 4 August, the last day of her second cruise for Transocean, she ran aground in just 4 metres of water in the Oresund Sound between Denmark and Sweden. It was later discovered that she had been between 150 to 200 metres outside the correct channel. For her 600 passengers this was the end of their cruise, they had to be taken from the ship and returned home from Copenhagen. Meanwhile divers were sent to inspect the hull of the ship, and it appeared at the time that all that was damaged was her dignity. Swedish tugs were in attendance to help in the refloating efforts once her bunkers had been discharged. However, despite all attempts she remained firmly stuck for several days. It was not until 9 p.m. on 7 August, with the aid of five tugs and with the ship using her own power that she was pulled free. Having arrived at a shipyard in Helsingborg a further inspection revealed that she had suffered some damage to a propeller. The repairs were carried out at the Lloyd Werft yard at Bremerhaven and having missed only one cruise of her schedule she returned to service on 18 August.

Despite this rather inauspicious beginning Transocean were sufficiently happy with *Gripsholm/Sagafjord* to express interest not in extending the charter but in buying her outright: but they were unable – or perhaps unwilling – to meet the high price that Cunard were asking for the ship. However, Transocean were not the only company who were interested in acquiring her, for despite having generated some unfortunate headlines during 1996, her reputation was largely intact.

On 23 October it was announced that she had been sold to Saga Shipping, a subsidiary of the Saga Group, the UK company that specialises in holidays for older people, for $19.23 million. Saga, which had traditionally just marketed space on ships of other companies, had said that demand for cruises was so high that in order to guarantee a consistent supply of high quality accommodation they felt the need to buy their own ship. Saga was already filling fourteen per cent of the berths available in the UK market at the time. Once her charter to Transocean, as *Gripsholm*, was at an end *Sagafjord* was to be delivered to Saga Holidays in the spring of 1997. Saga announced that she would undergo a refit and would be renamed *Saga Rose*. Her home port would be Dover and that her cruises would be marketed to the over 50's age group.

Sagafjord as *Gripsholm*…

…at Tilbury on 28 August 1996.

Vistafjord catches the sun in Grand Harbour, Valletta.

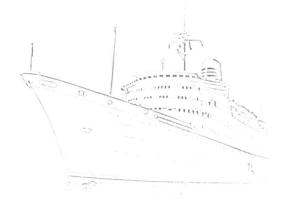

CHAPTER SEVEN

Vistafjord alone

Although *Vistafjord* was scheduled to undergo a $10 million refit at the Malta Drydock Company during April 1997 rumours persisted that Cunard were poised to dispose of her, and her fleet mate *Royal Viking Sun*. The German travel company Neckermann, which for many years had very successfully operated the Russian cruise ship *Maxim Gorkiy*, were cited as being a potential buyer. Other reports said that none other than Saga were interested in acquiring her: this, however, was firmly denied. The chairman of Princess Cruises had said that he thought the whole Cunard Line operation was not saleable: that their ships were all too old and needed to be replaced. Nevertheless, both he, and the executives at the Carnival Corporation said that they would consider buying the Line – if the price was right. Those comments, and the rumours, were particularly interesting when compared to the statement issued by the chairman of Cunard just a few months earlier. He had denied the rumours that Cunard might soon be sold, stating: "There is no need to sell Cunard." He went on to say that the Line was comfortable with its current fleet but that a possible expansion may be considered towards the end of the year. The rumours regarding the disposal of *Vistafjord* appeared to be groundless and she continued with her planned itineraries. Unfortunately though, she was suddenly thrust into the spotlight once again.

She had departed Fort Lauderdale on 5 April 1997, heading for the Mediterranean (it was after this cruise that she would undergo the scheduled refit in Malta). In the early hours of the following morning her passengers were woken by the sound of the emergency alarms and were instructed to gather on the open Promenade Deck. A fire had apparently broken out in a corridor near to the laundry and as a result there was a lot of smoke in the area of the passenger and crew accommodation. Her lifeboats were lowered to the boarding position but fortunately it did not become necessary to evacuate the ship. Sadly, a crew member died of smoke inhalation. With the fire extinguished *Vistafjord* turned back towards the Bahamas and docked at Freeport. Once the damage was assessed it was decided that the cruise should be abandoned. The ship was then cleaned of the damage caused by the fire, smoke and water and she sailed, without passengers, for Malta.

Unfortunately, another small fire resulted in the cancellation of her first cruise scheduled after the refit.

The following Spring the announcement was made that a deal had been struck between Kvaerner and the Carnival Corporation for the purchase of Cunard Line, with Carnival having a sixty-six per cent share in the company. *Vistafjord*'s future in the fleet appeared to be assured with the president of the company emphasising the fact that there was a long-term future for both her and the *Queen Elizabeth 2*. There was more than just a hint that *Vistafjord* might be renamed *Caronia* and even the suggestion that she might reintroduce the distinctive pale green livery that the former *Caronia* had been so famous for. Rumours of her disposal from the fleet faded along with the memories of those unfortunate incidents just a few months earlier. Suddenly, with the might of the Carnival Corporation behind it Cunard began to reacquire its former status. There was talk, serious talk, of new ships.

While there were many ship enthusiasts who greeted the idea of *Vistafjord* being renamed *Caronia* with enthusiasm there were probably many more of her loyal passengers who asked "Why?" As the many new cruise ships entering the market had appeared to be in a competition to be larger, with more balconies, more on board diversions and more of everything, *Vistafjord* had sailed serenely on as the very epitome of an elegant cruise ship. To change her was seen as unnecessary. Nevertheless, towards the end of 1998 Cunard announced that in November 1999, fifty years after the Line had taken delivery of *Caronia*, the cruising liner that affectionately became known as the 'Green Goddess', the new Cunard Line Limited (as the company was now restyled) would introduce a "new" *Caronia* to the fleet. Following a major refurbishment *Vistafjord* would emerge from the shipyard sporting "traditional Cunard livery". Unfortunately, this did not mean a re-introduction of those delicate shades of green (which in fact would have probably been more than her loyal passengers could have coped with). Instead a computer-generated image was presented showing the ship with a charcoal-grey hull. While elegant, it was a look that evoked the traditional image of a Cunard

Vistafjord at Southampton with *Kazakstan II*…

Atlantic liner rather than one of its cruising liners. *Vistafjord*'s career as "the new" *Caronia* was scheduled to begin on 18 December.

Cunard launched what appeared to be a masterly advertising campaign, which emphasised the "timeless elegance … and gracious atmosphere." The Line was not seeking to be all things to all cruise passengers but to recapture the elegance and mystique of ocean travel. The company's chief executive said: "While most of the cruise industry is trying to differentiate itself from the formality of classic cruising we feel there is a niche for us, where people still desire the graciousness and elegance that has always been our tradition." The Line were at great pains not to lose those passengers that had become so very fond of *Vistafjord*, these words were meant as an assurance that all would be well and remain unchanged. A pity therefore that close inspection of a stylish brochure, announcing "A Modern Classic", revealed that the former North Cape Bar would become the Golden Lion Pub!

Vistafjord's final cruise was a 12-night trip from Southampton to Spain, Madeira, the Canary Islands and Portugal. On completion of the cruise, on 20 November,

Vistafjord sailed to the Lloyd Werft shipyard at Bremerhaven to undergo a $5 million transformation that would turn her into the 'new' *Caronia*. The redesign was carried out under the direction of Tilberg Design, the company that had also been in charge of her 1995 refitting. The Viking Club became the Piccadilly Club and the restaurant was renamed the Franconia dining room. Someone at Cunard had probably realised that the Golden Lion Pub hardly set the right sort of tone, the room, which after all is the principal cocktail bar on the ship, was re-named the White Star Bar.

With the work completed the 'new' *Caronia* left Bremerhaven on 7 December for Britain, the short trip being marketed as a mini-cruise offering potential passengers a taste of *Caronia* 1990s style. Sadly, it was a stormy crossing, the heavy seas meant that the outer decks were closed off to passengers and for many it was a far from enjoyable experience. It was in Liverpool on 10 that a re-naming ceremony took place, in the presence of hundreds of people. She was berthed at the Pier Head in front of the original Cunard building, which flew the Cunard flag again for the first time in many years. During the ceremony, the Deputy

...and with the *Queen Elizabeth 2*.

Prime Minister, John Prescott, who had once upon a time been a steward aboard Cunard's Canadian ships, announced the re-flagging, in the near future, of the *Caronia* under the British register as a result of the government's new tonnage tax. Pam Conover, President and chief executive officer of Cunard acted as the new godmother of the ship: *Vistafjord* was now officially *Caronia.* The whole event ended with a tremendous fireworks display.

At the conclusion of the re-naming ceremony *Caronia* sailed to Southampton: there she boarded passengers for a Caribbean Millennium Cruise, calling at the Azores, St Kitts, Dominica, St Lucia, Barbados and Madeira. *Caronia* was at anchor, with the *Queen Elizabeth 2*, off Bridgetown, Barbados on 31 December 1999 for the New Year's Eve party and fireworks display.

It was not long after *Caronia* had re-entered service that an announcement was made that she would have to be temporarily withdrawn from service, between 18 May and 3 June 2000 in order that her stability be improved. The work would again be carried out at the Lloyd Werft shipyard. Over the years several additions

had been made to her superstructure, including two-deck high penthouse suites forward of the funnel. It appeared that she no longer conformed to international stability requirements. The time scale for the refit turning *Vistafjord* into *Caronia* did not allow for this additional work to be done, so temporary ballast was added to her bottom tanks. It seemed very likely that sponsons would have to be added to her hull. These would have been an addition that would have undoubtedly compromised her lovely lines. As it turned out sponsons were not added, instead the ballast was made more permanent.

Caronia's cruise programme was very similar to that of previous years: Scandinavia and the Mediterranean in the summer and then during the winter months she would sail on longer and more distant itineraries, for example in 2001 she undertook a series of cruises between Rio de Janeiro and Fort Lauderdale and vice versa, sailing mostly along the west coast of South America. On the first of these cruises, while cruising the Chilean fjords, she encountered her near sister, *Saga Rose*. She had only been sailing for a few brief months as *Caronia* before the

Above: A classic line up, *Vistafjord* in Istanbul, astern of her is the Turkish liner *Akdeniz*.

Left: Touching up the paintwork.

Above right: *Vistafjord* transformed. Refitted in Bremerhaven, she prepares to sail for Britain where she was officially re-named *Caronia* at Liverpool.

Right: *Caronia* sailing from Barcelona.

...alongside at Bridgetown, Barbados.

Caribbean cruising...

rumours about her possible sale began again. Once more Saga were cited as being interested but at the time there was some indication that the company might be poised to place an order for a new ship instead.

On 18 September 2001 Cunard announced that as part of their long-term strategy to capture a larger share of the British cruise market they would be basing *Caronia* on cruises out of Southampton from May 2002, operating cruises from between 5 and 21-days. The president and chief executive officer of the Line, Pam Conover, said: "It makes perfect sense for us to dedicate a vessel to the UK market ..." Given that P&O's very popular *Victoria* (which had been built as the Swedish America Line's *Kungsholm*) was due to leave the British market later in 2001 it certainly did make perfect sense for Cunard to step in with their similarly-styled and similarly-sized *Caronia* – indeed it was the obvious thing to do! Three months after making this announcement Cunard's parent company, the Carnival Corporation, announced that they had signed a letter of intent with the Italian ship building company, Fincantieri, for the construction of a 1,968-passenger, 85,000grt cruise ship specifically designed to serve the British market. At that time she was scheduled for delivery in January 2005 (although this would later be revised). It was obvious from this statement alone that *Caronia's* time as part of the Cunard fleet was short. Although having enthused over her classic style and her aura of exclusivity, with capacity for just 650 passengers, it was all too apparent that Cunard's marketing effort would be all for the new ship: to be named *Queen Victoria*. Serried ranks of balconies, vast show lounges and a soaring atrium would all win out over the quiet and refined elegance of the former Norwegian flagship.

Beauty and the beast. *Caronia* is dwarfed by the vast *Costa Fortuna* at Funchal.

Still as *Caronia* but by this time already sold to Saga.

Nevertheless, *Caronia* was for a while longer still a Cunard ship and her transfer to the British market appeared to work very well. She quickly became a favourite British cruise ship and was seen by some as restoring the grand tradition of British luxury cruising. She even presented a rather more traditional look that the much lamented *Victoria*, whose near perfect profile had been sadly disfigured by P&O on her introduction to their fleet 23 years earlier. As a consequence, *Caronia* still managed to attract passengers from the United States who appreciated her quiet and dignified style.

As was expected, her career as *Caronia* was to be brief. On 30 May 2003, after what had in fact been years of rumour and counter-rumour Saga Holidays Ltd announced that they had bought the ship and that she would join the company in spring 2005 after undergoing a major refit. In a letter to all former Saga passengers the company stated: "When *Saga Rose* was first introduced, six years ago, the response was tremendous. Since then, to cater for the growing demand for high quality, great value cruising, we have chartered a second ship, *Saga Pearl* (which had formerly been the Swan Hellenic ship *Minerva*) and are now pleased to introduce a third ship."

Although Saga had bought the ship, *Caronia* was to maintain her already announced programme of cruises through the rest of the year and through most of 2004. There was considerable speculation as to what her new name would be. On several occasions during the summer of 2004 as *Caronia* cruised the Fjords, the Baltic and the Mediterranean, people who were very obviously not passengers, could be seen carrying clipboards and tape measures about the ship. As discreetly as possible she was being measured up. Saga had big plans for the *Caronia*.

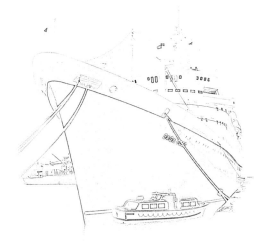

CHAPTER EIGHT

The Saga Sisters

The sale of the *Saga Rose* to the Saga Group Ltd, was completed while the ship was in Malta. She then sailed from there for Southampton. The announcement of the name, *Saga Rose*, which although a clever twist on her original name as well as that of her owners, did not at first meet with favour with many industry watchers.

On 16 April 1997 the A&P Group issued a Press Release that announced the Saga Group Ltd had awarded A&P Southampton the contract to carry out an extensive two part refit programme on the *Saga Rose*, the Company's new cruise ship. The Press Release stated: "The *Saga Rose*, three times winner of the title 'Cruise Ship of the Year' (under her former name, *Sagafjord*) will be restored to her former glory as a 5-star vessel, placing her in the upper echelons of the world cruise market."

The contract involved the *Saga Rose* spending two periods in A&P Southampton's King George V dry dock during 1997. Phase one had already begun, on 15 April, and lasted four weeks. The work involved a total refurbishment of the ship's public areas as well as some technical work. The Press Release stated that the second phase of the work, which was due to last for 8 weeks, was to follow in late October, when as well as further improvements to the public spaces the cabins would all be given a major upgrade and work would be done in order that the ship complied with new safety requirements. In all, the two refits would cost Saga £15 million.

Commenting on the award of the contract, Roger De Haan, Chairman of Saga Group Ltd, said, "We are delighted to have been able to award the contract to a British yard and are sure our customers will endorse this decision. We are please to be working with a number of UK-based suppliers, including A&P Southampton, in what is a move of major importance to Saga."

David Adams, the managing director of A&P Southampton said, "The combination of our price competitiveness and proven track record has, in my view, given us a winning edge in securing this contract against tough competition from elsewhere in Europe." Several months before the yard had successfully completed a refit of the *Queen Elizabeth 2* on time, and this had been followed by four other major cruise ship contracts.

Saga Rose emerged from her initial refit looking very different and very smart, and there were many who were of the view that she had in fact never looked better. Her hull was now dark blue and her funnel was quite a deep yellow with a narrow white band and a dark blue top. Somehow, the dark hull appeared to give the ship greater visual balance, lessening the heaviness caused by the shadows created by the balconied cabins on the top of her superstructure. Internally she also had a new look and it was one that was wholly in harmony with her classic style. Out had gone the somewhat unsympathetic metal-framed furniture that had been installed by Cunard in some of the public rooms; in their place was furniture of an altogether more sumptuous look. Overall she still retained an aura of her original Scandinavian elegance, albeit that in some places she was decorated in a style that was more suited to British tastes, inevitably so of course. She arrived in Dover on 14 May and undertook a 3-day shakedown cruise before departing on the 20th on her first cruise for Saga, to the Mediterranean. Many of her cruises were fully booked and there was every indication that *Saga Rose* would again become a very popular ship. Unfortunately, it appeared that her earlier woes were still not behind her, for during her first months of service *Saga Rose* was dogged by a variety of problems. This of course generated some bad publicity and resulted in various rumours circulating, some of which implied that the problems were a result of poor maintenance during her previous months of service. The press played up these misfortunes, which was not at all helpful. Nevertheless, *Saga Rose* was fortunate to have a very dedicated crew and gradually these problems seemed largely to be overcome. Perhaps on the strength of her former, almost legendary reputation, as well as the enthusiastic reports from her new passengers her cruises continued to be well booked: thus confounding the critics who had thought Saga were reckless in the acquisition of a ship of their own.

A fire, caused by either an electrical fault or a welding spark, broke out aboard *Saga Rose* at 2 p.m. on Sunday 14 December while she was still in dry dock at Southampton undergoing the second stage of her extensive refit. Although it took several hours to extinguish and produced a lot of smoke there were no flames and the damage was limited to wiring, and to a small number of cabins at the forward end of her promenade deck superstructure. This unfortunately meant that her Christmas cruise, on which she had been scheduled to depart the following weekend, was cancelled so that repairs could be completed in time for her World Cruise departure on 7 January 1998. *Saga Rose* had been scheduled to sail from Dover but instead she was forced to begin her world cruise from Southampton. Severe storms in the area of the Dover Straits would have made it difficult for her to safely clear the harbour. Bad luck continued to follow the ship during the cruise and several ports had to be dropped due to various mechanical problems. Her air conditioning failed for several days and plumbing problems caused flooding to some cabins. Again, it was the dedication of her crew that ensured these problems were overcome and as a result the cruise was largely considered to be a success.

The World Cruise became a very important part of *Saga Rose's* cruise calendar; it was always of at least 100-days duration, and the Millennium World Cruise was of 114-days. Usually on about 4 January she departs from Southampton on a westward route towards the Caribbean, through the Panama Canal, across the Pacific calling at various remote and exotic islands, onward to New Zealand, Australia and Indonesia. The cruise continuing across the Indian Ocean with calls at both Sri Lanka and India before heading into the Red Sea, through the Suez Canal and into the Mediterranean, arriving back in Southampton in early-mid-April. While following largely a similar route each year there are diversions. The Millennium World Cruise included calls in Japan and China as well as Vietnam. On the 2001 World Cruise *Saga Rose* voyaged down to Brazil and Argentina instead of heading for the Caribbean, giving her passengers the opportunity not only the chance to see the exciting cities of Rio and Buenos Aires but also the Falkland Islands and Punta Arenas and the Chilean fjords. On other occasions, instead of returning to Europe by the Suez Canal *Saga Rose's* itinerary has included ports on East, South and West Africa. A real highlight was the 2004 World Cruise, it included *Saga Rose's* first ever visit to the Antarctic. She made a call at the Falkland Islands on 26 January before heading south to the Antarctic Peninsula. For three consecutive days her passengers had the opportunity to travel ashore in 'zodiacs' (which had been especially purchased for the Antarctic visit). To ensure that they were suitably dressed for the trips, each passenger was supplied with a protective red jacket, waterproof trousers and red Wellington boots – as well as an inflatable life jacket. On the first day, passengers landed on Half Moon Island, part of the South Shetlands. On the second they visited Waterboat Point, part of the mainland, and on the third day the ship took them to Deception Island where *Saga Rose* actually entered into the rim of a volcano. It was on Deception Island that some passengers took the remarkable opportunity to swim in the thermally-heated water from a lava beach! The days spent at this isolated area of the World was regarded by most of the passengers as the very best part of the entire cruise, and it was included as part of the 2005 World Cruise itinerary.

The World Cruise attracts many passengers back year after year, a large number of them making the whole circumnavigation: while many others chose to take the lengthy segments. However, it is not just with the World Cruise that *Saga Rose* has become such a familiar and well-loved part of the British cruise market. The first cruise on her return from the voyage around the World is often a three weeks cruise in the Mediterranean, the early and mid-summer months finds *Saga Rose* cruising the waters of what must surely be her spiritual home; Scandinavia, the Norwegian fjords, North Cape, Spitzbergen and Iceland, even to Greenland. On the later summer months she returns to the Mediterranean and to the ever-popular Atlantic Islands. Some years her Christmas and New Year cruise will be an extended trip, maybe for as long as a month, across to the Caribbean.

In many respects *Saga Rose* continues a very similar pattern of cruises to those she has operated throughout her life. Longer cruises; for her a cruise of two weeks is the norm and a three-week cruise is far from unusual, and with these cruises she has built up a loyal following. She has been described as being the nearest that we have today to the legendary cruise ship of the 1950s and 1960s: the *Andes* of Royal Mail Line. However, far from emulating the legendary status of a liner of the past, *Saga Rose* has become a cruising legend in her own right.

On her 2001 World Cruise *Saga Rose* stood proudly at anchor off Easter Island. She gleamed in the sunshine as her passengers, returning from their trips ashore, jostled for the best vantage point to photograph her from the after end of the launch. The sweeping bow appeared to soar above the little boat. "Oh! Oh! Just look at her; we don't care if she is 36-years old, she is just beautiful - and we love her!" Enthused a female passenger. It was perhaps not quite the kind of outburst one might have expected from a Saga passenger but it was a sentiment that everyone agreed with.

For five years *Saga Rose* maintained this schedule of cruises, "Classic Cruising" as Saga called it, in solitary splendour. Such was the success of this formula that Saga Holidays had seen there was a need for a second vessel. Several ships had been considered but none had really been suitable, for various reasons. Then, in the Spring of 2002 P&O announced that they would be replacing their almost new vessel, *Minerva*, which had entered service for their Swan Hellenic Cruises subsidiary in 1996, with a much larger vessel. Thus, the 12,500-gt *Minerva* was suddenly available. Her modest size, capacity for just 352 passengers and her elegantly traditional public rooms and cabins made her very attractive to Saga. The company announced that she had been chartered, and would sail exclusively for them between April and October 2003 as the *Saga Pearl*.

While *Saga Rose* continued with her usual programme of cruises the *Saga Pearl* made her first cruise with the company beginning on 1 May with a cruise from the Mediterranean to Britain. During that first year she operated cruises as far afield as Greenland and Brazil. The charter was extended to 2004 and a very similar programme was operated again, although in this year it was *Saga Rose* that operated the cruise up to Greenland.

Saga Rose at anchor off St Helena...

...in the King George V drydock at Southampton...

...being made ready...

...to begin her career with Saga.

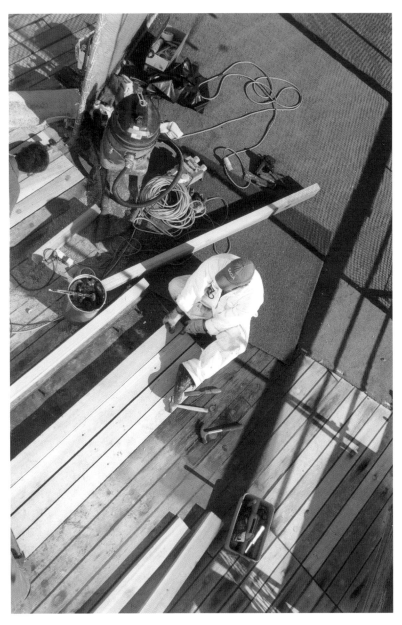

Maintenance is unending to keep a classic liner in prime condition.

Saga Rose anchored off Easter Island.

Saga had announced on 30 May 2003 their acquisition of Cunard's *Caronia*, the near-sister to *Saga Rose*. *Saga Pearl* was, therefore, a stop-gap vessel, a suitable ship to get their customer base used to the idea of a two-ship fleet and of a wider choice of cruises. It was probably just by coincidence that the announcement by Saga, that they had bought the *Caronia,* all-but coincided with the 30th anniversary of her 'maiden arrival' in New York (on 31 May 1973) as *Vistafjord*.

As *Caronia* entered her final season of cruises with Cunard the speculation regarding her new name intensified. The name *Saga Star* was suggested early on and for a long time it seemed very likely that it would be the name chosen. Then word came from the Saga headquarters that Roger De Haan, the Saga Holidays Chairman, had said that the ship's name did not have to have a Saga prefix at all! However, on a cruise aboard *Saga Rose* Mr De Haan, speaking to a gathering of passengers, suggested the name *Saga Orchid*. It was not at all well received. Then in May 2004 the announcement was made - she would be named *Saga Star*. The choice was not met with universal acclaim but it was largely regarded as being

'OK'. Within a couple of days this was followed by a further announcement stating that she would in fact be named *Saga Ruby*. Apparently, *Saga Star* had been the name of a particularly down-market ferry that the Saga organisation was anxious to distance itself from. It was also at this time that Saga confirmed that they would no longer operate the *Saga Pearl* once her 2004 cruise programme was ended.

It was announced that *Saga Ruby* would undergo extensive, £17 million, refurbishment in dry dock, which was planned to take place between November 2004 and January 2005. The substantial contract for the refit was awarded to Malta Shipyards Limited following an extensive and competitive bidding process involving several European shipyards. Mivan, the Northern Ireland-based international contractor won the contract to outfit the ship. While much of the work was to be pre-assembled at Mivan's joinery workshops in Antrim, the completed sections were then shipped to Malta. By 1 October 2005 most passenger ships must be equipped with an approved sprinkler system. A Hi-Fog system with two diesel-driven pump units feeding over 2,400 sprinklers, to protect all the accommodation

A World Cruise highlight...

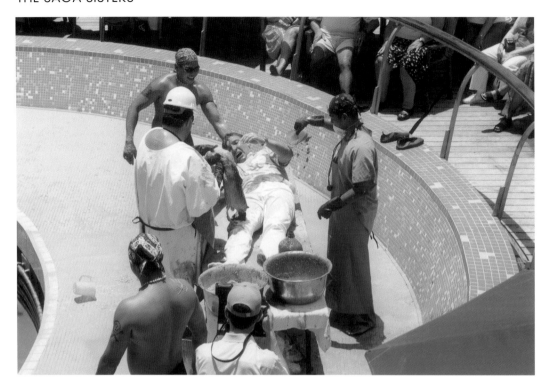

...the Crossing of the Line ceremony.

and machinery spaces, was one of the most important, and indeed essential, parts of the extensive refitting work.

On 20 October she departed Southampton for the last time as a Cunard ship, on her farewell cruise as *Caronia*. She returned on 1 November and after having off-loaded items belonging to Cunard she then set sail for Malta and arrived there on the 7th. It was then that she was formally handed over to Saga. Work began immediately to prepare the ship for what would be the most extensive refit of her life.

Several months before the ship had ceased sailing for Cunard, Saga naturally began marketing the cruises to be operated by *Saga Ruby*, the brochures and other lavish publicity material detailing the extensive amount of work they were planning. It was very obvious that many lessons had been learned from the years of operating *Saga Rose*. A most significant change involved the entire redesign of her lido deck and the re-positioning of her pool further aft. This was done in order that the Lido Café could be significantly enlarged, allowing a much more spacious area for passengers to enjoy a more casual breakfast and lunch. Up on Sun Deck what had been *Caronia's* Tivoli Restaurant would be transformed into the exclusive 30-seat View Restaurant, it was described as being *Saga Ruby's* "chic alternative to her Dining Room", the bar below it being refurbished, and

wittily re-named Preview. All of the public rooms and cabins were refurbished. It would be the most dramatic and extensive refitting of the ship since she was built. Whilst *Saga Rose* was regarded as being very elegantly traditional, for *Saga Ruby* a whole new look was being aimed for. "Contemporary elegance" was the phrase that was used in a lavish brochure devoted purely to the refit, inspired by traditional designs the furnishings and décor of the public rooms were to have a contemporary twist. The designs for the interior being created by Alison Clixby of Clixby Associates, a company that had already done work aboard *Saga Rose* and other cruise ships. Whilst a great deal of the transformation of *Caronia* into *Saga Ruby* was centred on her public spaces considerable work was also done behind the scenes. As well as the installation of the new sprinkler system both her main engines and all of the generators and boilers were dismantled for complete over-hauls. Her hull was sandblasted back to the bare steel before being given her new dark-blue livery. Then, on 27 January 2005, resplendent in the late afternoon sun, *Saga Ruby* was floated out from the drydock, and was made ready for the voyage to Southampton. Workmen remained on board to continue with the task of fitting out the ship. She arrived, without fanfare, on Monday 7 February and was berthed alongside the Mayflower Cruise Terminal: the fitting out work continued.

The Lido Deck aboard *Saga Rose* has remained unchanged throughout her career.

Another exotic port beckons.

From the Bridge wing.

The Bridge aboard *Saga Rose*.

Even *Saga Rose*'s tenders have classic lines.

On Friday 25 February *Saga Ruby* was made ready for a brief shakedown cruise, with specially invited guests aboard, across to the Belgian port of Zeebrugge. Before she departed a very low-key naming ceremony took place in the Ballroom. The Bishop of Southampton gave a blessing on the ship and then Virginia Goodsell (the wife of Andrew Goodsell, the Chief Executive of the Saga Group Ltd) performed the actual re-naming. *Saga Ruby* was back alongside at Southampton on the 27th with the finishing touches being made to her public rooms and newly created lido deck.

On 1 March 2005, just two months short of the thirty second anniversary of her entering service as *Vistafjord*, *Saga Ruby* departed from Southampton on her maiden voyage under the Saga house flag: a 32-night cruise to the Azores, the Caribbean and Bermuda. Her first passengers had begun boarding early that afternoon: they were the first to encounter the transformation that had been created by Alison Clixby. "Contemporary elegance" had been the phrase used in the early publicity material used to promote *Saga Ruby* and that was most certainly what they were greeted with. The whole length of her Veranda Deck (where the main public rooms are located) was a unified feel of style and colour: burgundy, pale gold, ivory, bronze, grey, terracotta, pale green and yellow. The whole effect was rich, luxurious and understated - really quite masculine (as opposed to the more feminine feel of *Saga Rose*) and in each room there were striking and dramatic modern artworks.

It appeared that Saga of today had their eyes very firmly on what would be attractive to the passengers of tomorrow.

The two former Norwegian America Line flagships are once again united: a fact that became all the more apparent when the two ships met for the first time as Saga Sisters on 20 July in Dover. The *Saga Ruby* preparing to depart on a 14-night cruise: to Dublin, around Iceland, the Faroes and Shetlands and Norway. The *Saga Rose*, also heading for Iceland but by an easterly route. By November 2004 Saga had announced that both ships would operate World Cruises in 2006. Although they will sail on quite different itineraries: the *Saga Rose* sailing on a westward route that would first take her to South America, and the *Saga Ruby* on an eastward route towards South Africa. Both ships would leave Southampton at the same time, 9.30 p.m. on 4 January and sail in tandem as far as Funchal, having arrived together after celebrating New Year together in the Azores.

The legend of the Saga Sisters continues ....

The Promenade Deck.

AFTER-DINNER GAYETY — Focal point of night-time activity is the elegantly appointed Main Lounge, where passengers gather after a satisfying dinner to enjoy the ship's social functions, to listen to sprightly music, and to dance. There is a stage, and a screen for showings of select sound films.

Top: The Main Lounge aboard *Oslofjord*...

Above: ...and the Ballroom aboard *Sagafjord* when new. Similar scenes are enacted every day aboard *Saga Rose* and *Saga Ruby*.

Top: The Britannia Lounge aboard *Saga Rose*.

Above: The Foyer and Main Staircase aboard *Bergensfjord*.

Sagafjord continued the trend.

LADIES' LOUNGE - TOURIST CLASS - LIBRARY

Left: *Bergensfjord*'s Ladies Lounge and Tourist Class Library.

Top right: The Library...

Bottom right: ...and Writing Room aboard *Sagafjord*.

Below: Still a popular spot aboard *Saga Rose*.

Top left: The North Cape Bar as it originally appeared in all its Scandinavian simplicity...

Left: ...and the bar today – still very elegant but a little cosier.

Top right: The original design for the Garden Lounge aboard *Sagafjord*...

Above: ...and as the room appeared when she first entered service as *Saga Rose*.

The original design for the Lido Deck…

…and the Lido as it is now.

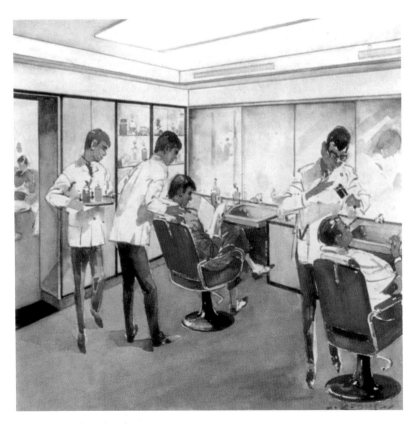

Sagafjord's Barber Shop.

and Beauty Parlour.

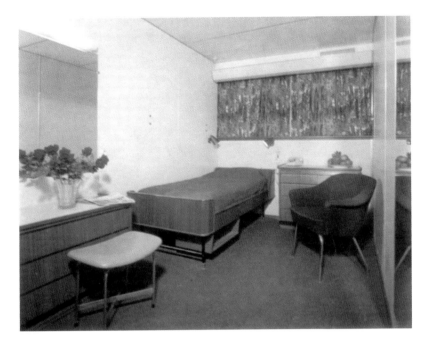

Some of *Sagafjord*'s original artwork remains in place aboard *Saga Rose*.

Top: A Single Cabin aboard *Sagafjord*.

Above: A Double Cabin aboard *Saga Rose*.

The original design for *Sagafjord*'s Dining Room.

Tenders being made ready...

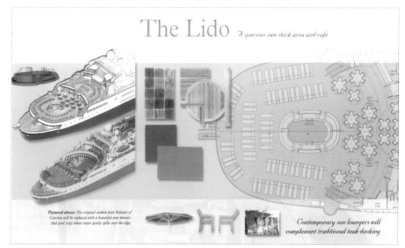

...for going ashore.

Top right: Lavish publicity material to introduce *Saga Ruby*.

Middle right: The after decks of the former *Vistafjord* totally redesigned.

Bottom right: *Saga Ruby* – a whole new career ahead of her.

Top: In brilliant sunshine at Southampton the finishing touches are made.

Above: The newly redesigned Lido Deck.

Top: The Library.

Above: The Dining Room – just waiting for the linen, china, silverware and glass to complete the picture.

The dramatic Main Staircase.

Right above: Proud in Saga colours.

Right below: On 28 February 2005, almost ready to embark her first passengers.

Above; The South Cape Bar.

Above right: The Ballroom.

Right: The redesigned Lido Café.

Appendix

The grey market is the market for goods and service for older members of society (those whose hair is going or has gone gray). While many companies have sought to exploit and expand into the youth market there is an increasing awareness that the grey market is also well worth examining.

As patterns of living and work have changed so has the relationship between the age groups. Many people are either retiring early to enjoy leisure activities or to seek a career change. There is also less pressure on parents to provide an inheritance for their children especially where the latter are in well-paid posts. Increasingly, the grey market has growing levels of disposable income and many seem intent on spending a fair proportion of their wealth while they can still enjoy it.

In 1951, Sidney De Haan, who was based in Folkestone, Kent, realised that retired people would appreciate the opportunity to take lower-cost seaside holidays outside of the main and thus more expensive holiday periods. The main holiday periods coincide with school vacations and thus hoteliers and tour operators tend to offer discounts for those who are willing to take their holidays outside of these busy times. The first vacation De Haan offered cost £6 10s and included full board, travel to the resort and three excursions.

Many in the holiday business scoffed at De Haan's decision to target a particular niche market but De Haan's holidays became more and more popular and the ability (due to an arrangement between the UK and France at the time) to travel on day trips between the UK and France without a passport led De Haan to fly to Le Touquet from 1959. This was at a time when most British holiday makers took their breaks at UK resorts and when few had actually travelled by aircraft except on military service.

So successful was this first foreign endeavor that in 1960 De Haan pioneered tourism in the Algarve on the Atlantic coast of Portugal, establishing the Aldeia do Mar Turistica Holiday Complex at Albufeira.

Saga's customer base grew rapidly and in 1966 the Saga Club was launched with members receiving *Saga News*, the forerunner to the current *Saga Magazine*. At the time the age criteria for booking a Saga vacation was sixty – the age that women received the UK State pension.

From the early 1970s, Saga was also offering vacations to Romania, Spain and Yugoslavia with a US operation based in Boston commencing in 1979. By the end of 1981, US seniors were also able to enjoy a Saga vacation.

By the time De Haan retired in 1984, the *Saga Magazine* had been launched, providing general information and articles to those over sixty. His son Roger took over the company and continued the tradition of finding out exactly what it was that the over-sixty market required from their vacations. It has been this customer-centred approach that has been the main reason for Saga's continuing success and growth.

The older members of society have always been amongst the safest drivers and have a reputation for being concerned about financial probity. In 1987 Saga Services was established to provide insurance, investment and other services for Saga customers. The *Saga Magazine* had become one of the UK's highest circulation magazines showing that Sidney De Haan was perfectly correct in deciding to provide his company's services to a niche market. As the number of older people has been growing steadily, it was in fact a very sensible market to target.

With the change in employment patterns and more and more people taking early retirement, the qualifying age was lowered from sixty to fifty in 1995, thus opening up a much larger potential market. The over-fifty market has traditionally been one of the strongest in the cruise industry. While many cruise companies offer family holidays there are still many over-fifties who take not one but two or more cruise per year

The older a holiday maker was the more safety and security were likely to feature as choice factors in booking a holiday; factors that are provided by cruise holidays. Saga Holidays began to book customers onto cruise ships operated by the main cruise operators but with an added extra. For those cruises for which Saga provided a booking service, the company sent a representative on board.

Given that Saga's level of involvement in cruising was increasing it did not surprise the holiday industry when, in 1996, Saga acquired the *Sagafjord* from Cunard and renamed the vessel *Saga Rose* and latterly purchased both the *Saga Ruby* and even more recently announced plans to acquire the *Spirit of Adventure* (ex-*Berlin*).

The Saga cruise product is designed around the needs of a customer base that is over fifty and comprises far more than just the cruise as it is a door to door experience.

Saga ships undertake cruises to the most popular cruising destinations for its predominantly but not exclusively UK clientele. In this respect Saga offer similar products to their main UK competitors for the middle-price-range cruise business, P&O and Cunard.

However, recognizing that a main attraction for the over-fifty age group is ease and security of travel, Saga provides not only accommodation, food and entertainment but also included in the price of the cruise are travel insurance and a no-tipping policy. The company also provides standard-class return rail fares or coach travel from the customer's home station to Dover or Southampton or to the airport for fly-cruises. There is also a private car service for customers living within seventy-five miles of the UK departure point

Saga ships have more dedicated single cabins than those of many companies providing a service for those who are traveling alone. it is clear from the high level of bookings and the amount of repeat business that what is offered is regarded not only as value for money but also meets the needs of the customer base to a considerable degree.

Food and entertainment are designed to appeal to an older age range too. The entertainment includes not only singers and comedians but also a number of specialist lecturers. Most cruise ships of the size of *Saga Rose* and *Saga Ruby* carry one or two specialist lecturers but the Saga ships often have as many as four on a cruise. This provides the customers with considerable choice as to how to fill their day. On a 2002 cruise up the coast of Norway and on to Longyearbyen (Spitzbergen), just 500 miles from the North Pole, the passengers received lectures during the days at sea from the ex-editor of the *Guinness Book of Records*, an ex-reporter and explorer, a Norwegian specialist and a maritime historian. That learning never ceases was shown by the fact that members of the 'University of the Third Age' were able to hold well-attended meetings on board the ship.

It is a proven fact that women tend to live longer than men and thus there are likely to be more single females than males on a Saga ship. Recognizing this, Saga is one of the few remaining cruise companies to provide two male dance hosts for the female customers.

Everything about the Saga experience has been done with the needs and wants of the customer base in mind. Saga have taken great care to meet the needs of their customers, even down to the provision of food and beverage items that reflect the lifestyle of the customer. It is little wonder that the company has been the subject of case studies on how to provide excellent customer care.

There is no casino on the Saga ships – it is not a customer requirement but the ships display a degree of comfort that one associates with a country house hotel or even one's own home. Comfort not glitz is perhaps more important after a certain time in life.

Saga's cruise business grew so much that that in 2002 it was announced that capacity was to be increased by chartering the 12,500grt *Minerva* (built on the hull of an incomplete ex-Soviet spy ship), with accommodation for 352 passengers, for six months per annum for three years with an option to cancel mid-way through the period (see later) to partner *Saga Rose*. The ship was renamed *Saga Pearl* and operated to the same high standard as *Saga Rose*.

Saga Pearl proved very popular and showed that Saga could expand its cruise operation. In 2004 it was announced that the *Saga Pearl* would be withdrawn in November 2004 and that Saga had acquired the semi-sister to *Saga Rose*, Cunard's *Caronia*. There was considerable speculation as to the name of the ship – the final choice of the company being *Saga Ruby*.

Other Saga enterprises have also grown. In 2000 Saga launched PrimeTime (the customer's Prime Time that is) digital radio and in October 2001 Saga 105.7FM hit the airwaves in the West Midlands of the UK.

Saga offers a wide range of holidays with some of the more adventurous tours particularly designed to appeal to more active travellers. Saga customers have (and are taking up in increasing numbers) opportunities to scuba dive in Mauritius, take a hot air balloon ride over the Masai Mara game reserve, live like a cowboy on a ranch in the US Wild West or ride an elephant through the jungle in Thailand

Saga Pearl

By 2002 *Saga Rose* was clearly an established component of the UK cruise market. The ship had a loyal following that was growing rapidly. It was clear to both Saga and commentators on the cruise industry that Saga Shipping was ripe for expansion.

Customers like a choice. *Saga Rose* still had plenty of life in her so rather than replace her with a larger vessel, Saga took the opportunity to expand incrementally by testing the market before making a major purchase. That the market testing was a success is shown by the purchase of *Caronia* to join *Saga Rose* and bring the sisters together again.

However, *Saga Pearl* served an important role in demonstrating that the over-fifty market in the UK could support two medium sized, dedicated vessels rather than just one. But, Saga have also discovered that the market can cope with more than two ships and *Saga Pearl*'s replacement is the *Spirit of Adventure*, previously the 9,500grt *Berlin* which was operating in the German market. This vessel joins *Saga Rose* and *Saga Ruby* in 2006 and will provide the company with another small ship to operate cruises to a similar variety of destinations as *Saga Pearl*.

The future looks bright for Saga. Doubtless *Saga Rose* will be the first of the sisters to go although not for some time yet. What will replace her – a brand new build, the first for Saga?

The *Berlin,* to become *Spirit of Adventure.*

Saga Pearl, Saga's stepping stone to a larger fleet.

Saga Ruby at Isafjordur, Iceland, July 2005.